BIOLOGICAL WARFARE

OPPOSING VIEWPOINTS®

BIOLOGICAL WARFARE

OPPOSING VIEWPOINTS®

Other Books of Related Interest

BIOLOGICAL WARFARE

OPPOSING VIEWPOINTS®

William Dudley, *Book Editor*

Daniel Leone, *President*
Bonnie Szumski, *Publisher*
Scott Barbour, *Managing Editor*
Helen Cothran, *Senior Editor*

OPPOSING
VIEWPOINTS®
SERIES

GREENHAVEN
PRESS®

THOMSON

GALE

San Diego • Detroit • New York • San Francisco • Cleveland
New Haven, Conn. • Waterville, Maine • London • Munich

© 2004 by Greenhaven Press. Greenhaven Press is an imprint of The Gale Group, Inc., a division of Thomson Learning, Inc.

Greenhaven® and Thomson Learning™ are trademarks used herein under license.

For more information, contact
Greenhaven Press
27500 Drake Rd.
Farmington Hills, MI 48331-3535
Or you can visit our Internet site at http://www.gale.com

Cover credit: © AP/Wide World Photos

LIBRARY OF CONGRESS CATALOGING-IN-PUBLICATION DATA

Biological warfare: opposing viewpoints / William Dudley, book editor.
   p. cm. — (Opposing viewpoints series)
Includes bibliographical references and index.
ISBN 0-7377-1671-1 (lib. bdg. : alk. paper) —
ISBN 0-7377-1672-X (pbk. : alk. paper)
   1. Biological warfare. 2. World politics—21st century. I. Dudley, William, 1964– . II. Opposing viewpoints series (Unnumbered)
UG447.8.B5653 2004
358'.38—dc21
                                                  2003042400

Printed in the United States of America

"Congress shall make
no law...abridging the
freedom of speech, or of
the press."

First Amendment to the U.S. Constitution

The basic foundation of our democracy is the First
Amendment guarantee of freedom of expression.
The Opposing Viewpoints Series is dedicated to the
concept of this basic freedom and the idea that it is
more important to practice it than to enshrine it.

Contents

Why Consider Opposing Viewpoints?

"The only way in which a human being can make some approach to knowing the whole of a subject is by hearing what can be said about it by persons of every variety of opinion and studying all modes in which it can be looked at by every character of mind. No wise man ever acquired his wisdom in any mode but this."

John Stuart Mill

In our media-intensive culture it is not difficult to find differing opinions. Thousands of newspapers and magazines and dozens of radio and television talk shows resound with differing points of view. The difficulty lies in deciding which opinion to agree with and which "experts" seem the most credible. The more inundated we become with differing opinions and claims, the more essential it is to hone critical reading and thinking skills to evaluate these ideas. Opposing Viewpoints books address this problem directly by presenting stimulating debates that can be used to enhance and teach these skills. The varied opinions contained in each book examine many different aspects of a single issue. While examining these conveniently edited opposing views, readers can develop critical thinking skills such as the ability to compare and contrast authors' credibility, facts, argumentation styles, use of persuasive techniques, and other stylistic tools. In short, the Opposing Viewpoints Series is an ideal way to attain the higher-level thinking and reading skills so essential in a culture of diverse and contradictory opinions.

In addition to providing a tool for critical thinking, Opposing Viewpoints books challenge readers to question their own strongly held opinions and assumptions. Most people form their opinions on the basis of upbringing, peer pressure, and personal, cultural, or professional bias. By reading carefully balanced opposing views, readers must directly confront new ideas as well as the opinions of those with whom they disagree. This is not to simplistically argue that everyone who reads opposing views will—or should—change his or her opinion. Instead, the series enhances readers' understanding of their own views by encouraging confrontation with opposing ideas. Careful examination of others' views can lead to the readers' understanding of the logical inconsistencies in their own opinions, perspective on why they hold an opinion, and the consideration of the possibility that their opinion requires further evaluation.

Evaluating Other Opinions

To ensure that this type of examination occurs, Opposing Viewpoints books present all types of opinions. Prominent spokespeople on different sides of each issue as well as well-known professionals from many disciplines challenge the reader. An additional goal of the series is to provide a forum for other, less known, or even unpopular viewpoints. The opinion of an ordinary person who has had to make the decision to cut off life support from a terminally ill relative, for example, may be just as valuable and provide just as much insight as a medical ethicist's professional opinion. The editors have two additional purposes in including these less known views. One, the editors encourage readers to respect others' opinions—even when not enhanced by professional credibility. It is only by reading or listening to and objectively evaluating others' ideas that one can determine whether they are worthy of consideration. Two, the inclusion of such viewpoints encourages the important critical thinking skill of objectively evaluating an author's credentials and bias. This evaluation will illuminate an author's reasons for taking a particular stance on an issue and will aid in readers' evaluation of the author's ideas.

It is our hope that these books will give readers a deeper understanding of the issues debated and an appreciation of the complexity of even seemingly simple issues when good and honest people disagree. This awareness is particularly important in a democratic society such as ours in which people enter into public debate to determine the common good. Those with whom one disagrees should not be regarded as enemies but rather as people whose views deserve careful examination and may shed light on one's own.

Thomas Jefferson once said that "difference of opinion leads to inquiry, and inquiry to truth." Jefferson, a broadly educated man, argued that "if a nation expects to be ignorant and free . . . it expects what never was and never will be." As individuals and as a nation, it is imperative that we consider the opinions of others and examine them with skill and discernment. The Opposing Viewpoints Series is intended to help readers achieve this goal.

David L. Bender and Bruno Leone,
Founders

Greenhaven Press anthologies primarily consist of previously published material taken from a variety of sources, including periodicals, books, scholarly journals, newspapers, government documents, and position papers from private and public organizations. These original sources are often edited for length and to ensure their accessibility for a young adult audience. The anthology editors also change the original titles of these works in order to clearly present the main thesis of each viewpoint and to explicitly indicate the opinion presented in the viewpoint. These alterations are made in consideration of both the reading and comprehension levels of a young adult audience. Every effort is made to ensure that Greenhaven Press accurately reflects the original intent of the authors included in this anthology.

Introduction

"Virtually every major technology has been exploited not only for peaceful purposes but also for hostile ones. Must this also happen with biotechnology, which is rapidly becoming the dominant technology of our age?"
—Matthew Meselson, New York Review of Books, December 20, 2001.

Biological warfare (also called germ or bacteriological warfare) is the use of living disease-causing agents such as viruses, germs, or fungi—or toxins derived from them—as a weapon of war against an enemy's soldiers, civilians, animals, or crops. Examples of potential biological agents include the smallpox virus and the bacterium *Yersinia pestis*, which causes plague. Such weapons could be used for either killing or incapacitating people. The term also refers to defensive measures against such attacks.

Biological weapons have been called the "poor nation's atomic bomb" because they could be developed by nations too poor to create or deploy nuclear or chemical weapons of mass destruction. Nuclear weapons require rare materials, and both nuclear and chemical weapons require significant scientific infrastructure to develop and deploy them. But biological weapons do not require rare materials, significant infrastructure, or esoteric knowledge. On the contrary, biological weapons can potentially be developed and even mass-produced by commercially available equipment found in many high school or college science classrooms. Actual germs can be purchased from universities and other institutions or derived from natural sources. The fact that so many different nations and groups possess the capability to create biological weapons makes it more probable that they will be used in the near future. Scientist Steven M. Block argues that "someone, somewhere, sometime seems bound to try something. . . . It would be tragic if it took the biological equivalent of Hiroshima to muster our response."

Biological warfare is a modern threat with a long history. Ancient peoples often placed corpses in the drinking wells of their enemies to gain a military advantage, or have thrown diseased bodies over city walls. One recorded case was the siege of the Crimean seaport of Caffa (now Fiodosia, Ukraine) in 1347. Mongol invaders used catapults to hurl dead bodies of plague victims into the walled city. When defenders of the city withdrew and fled to their home in Genoa, Italy, they took the disease with them; some historians blame the subsequent massive epidemic in Europe known as the Black Death on this biological attack. In another infamous case of biological warfare, British soldiers in North America in the 1700s used gifts of blankets to spread the smallpox disease to Native Americans.

These examples of biological warfare predate scientific understanding of how diseases are spread. In the nineteenth century, medical scientists developed the germ theory—the idea that contagious diseases are caused by microscopic infectious organisms. In the late 1800s microbiologists made significant advances in discovering and cultivating specific types of germs responsible for specific diseases, such as anthrax. These scientific advances would prove invaluable in treating and eradicating many diseases, but they also created the potential that such germs could be deliberately cultivated for use as weapons.

Germ theory was firmly established as the twentieth century began—a century that would experience two world wars, numerous other conflicts, and the invention and use of chemical and nuclear weapons. But in spite of science's new knowledge about how germs caused disease, the actual usage of them in warfare in the twentieth century has been relatively rare. In World War I, Germany tried to infect sheep destined for export to Russia with anthrax, while the French may have tried to infect German horses with a contagious disease called glanders. However, biological weapons played a very minor role compared with chemical and other weapons. In World War II biological weapons were used by Japan against Chinese targets. Although both Germany and the Allies researched and developed some biological weapons, these nations never used them during the war.

Biological weapons research programs begun during World War II by the United States, Great Britain, and the

Soviet Union continued after the war was over. During the long Cold War between the United States and the Soviet Union both sides traded unsubstantiated accusations of biological warfare. The United States was accused of using biological weapons in the Korean War—a charge the United States strongly denied, and which has never been proven. The Soviet Union was accused of biological warfare when a mysterious "yellow rain" appeared in Laos and Cambodia in the 1970s, but these charges have also lacked corroboration.

One reason why biological weapons may not have been used more often, despite the fact that many countries researched and stockpiled them, is that they could be a two-edged sword. Once a disease is introduced and begins to spread in a target human population, it may turn back on the attackers. Japanese efforts to spread cholera, plague, and other diseases in China were eventually stopped after they resulted in hundreds of deaths among Japan's own troops. Another reason that biological weapons have not been used is that they have long been stigmatized in the international community as being outside the norms of "civilized" warfare. Such an understanding was codified in the 1925 Geneva Protocol. Signatories of the protocol pledged not to wage biological warfare.

The perceived impracticality of biological weapons and the moral revulsion against their potential for mass casualties are among the reasons that the United States decided to renounce them in 1969. The United States stopped its biological weapons program and destroyed its stockpiles, which by then included agents that caused anthrax, botulism, tularemia, and other diseases (American research programs on biological warfare defenses continue to this day). Since 1972 more than one hundred nations have signed the Biological Weapons Convention, an international treaty that went beyond the 1925 Geneva Protocol by prohibiting the development and stockpiling of biological weapons and the means to deliver them.

Disturbing Developments

Despite the relative scarcity of biological warfare in the twentieth century, several developments have raised alarms for many that biological warfare may well be used sometime in the twenty-first century. One is the growing realization that the Biological Weapons Convention has not succeeded in its goals of weapons eradication. The Soviet Union, despite signing the BWC, created an impressively large biological weapons program in the 1970s and 1980s prior to the country's dissolution in 1991. The extent to which elements of the Soviet biological weapons complex are still operating in Russia (and perhaps making biological weapons technology available to other countries and groups) remains unknown. In the 1990s United Nations inspectors in Iraq uncovered evidence that that nation, another BWC signatory, had developed its own large biological weapons program. Other states believed to be aggressively pursuing biological weapons include Libya, North Korea, and Iran.

A second development raising concern about the possible use of biological weapons is the rise of terrorist groups that are not bound by the BWC or by norms governing countries. Some experts have argued that a "new breed" of terrorist has appeared in recent decades who is more willing to create mass casualties in ways unrelated to clear political goals. While traditional terrorist groups with negotiable political demands may avoid biological weapons as ultimately damaging to their cause, this new breed of terrorist may not. Terrorism expert and author Walter Laqueur writes, "The state of affairs is different with regard to terrorists of the lunatic fringe, certain religious fanatics, and terrorist groups that are not interested in negotiations but want to destroy the enemy *tout court*." Americans might not be comforted to know that one notable terrorist, al-Qaeda leader and alleged mastermind of the September 11, 2001, terrorist attacks, Osama bin Laden, has been quoted as saying that "we don't consider it a crime if we tried to have nuclear, chemical, biological weapons" in the holy war against the United States.

A third development concerning the threat of biological warfare is the continuing impressive advances in biological science and in biotechnology. "Modern bioscience has led to the development of many powerful tools for manipulating genes," writes scientist Block. "Such tools hold the key to revolutionary medical advances. . . . But they make equally

17

possible the creation of entirely new WMD [weapons of mass destruction], endowed with unprecedented power to destroy." Scientists can now not only isolate and cultivate germs and viruses, they can also change their genetic makeup. They can potentially be engineered to be more powerful, more easy to use, and more difficult to detect. Scientists can even theoretically design weapons to act against certain targeted ethnic groups by creating germs that attack particular genes or cell receptors found only in certain populations.

Whether or not these developments mean that the nightmare scenario of a large biological attack is now a likely possibility remains unknown. But journalist Madeline Drexler notes that U.S. experts on both sides of that question "do agree on two points: The threat of biological weapons is indisputably growing, and our public-health system would buckle under a massive epidemic." The viewpoints in this volume examine the prospective threat of biological warfare in the following chapters: How Serious a Danger Do Biological Weapons Pose? What Nations and Groups Constitute the Greatest Biological Warfare Threat? What Measures Should the United States Take to Prepare for Biological Warfare? How Can Biological Warfare Be Prevented? The contributors provide a diverse assortment of arguments responding to the disturbing possibility that advances in medicine and biology may be used for destructive ends.

CHAPTER 1

How Serious a Danger Do Biological Weapons Pose?

Chapter Preface

For Americans the year 2001 will be remembered as being dominated by two acts of terrorism. The September 11, 2001, attacks involved hijacked jetliners used as bombs to destroy the World Trade Center in New York City and damage the Pentagon in Washington, DC. The other incident—the October and November mailings of letters containing deadly anthrax powder to media and political figures—involved the use of a biological agent. The two incidents marked a new era of U.S. vulnerability to terrorism within its borders.

The question of which incident is a more alarming harbinger of the future is a matter of some debate. The anthrax mailings ultimately killed only five people (and left eighteen others sick)—a much lower number of fatalities than the estimated three thousand people who perished on September 11. Some observers cite this figure as evidence that biological weapons, whatever their potential lethality, are difficult agents to use in practice as weapons of mass destruction. However, the anthrax mailings were arguably just as alarming to Americans as the earlier attack. Part of America's government, including the House of Representatives, temporarily shut down amidst fears of more tainted letters. Many Americans expressed alarm at the prospect of simply opening their mail. "The psychological impact of a . . . biological weapon is much greater than the physical impact," notes terrorism expert Gary Eifried. "People understand explosions. They understand buildings collapsing. But they don't understand this. Not everyone lives in a tall building or flies on a plane. Everyone gets mail."

The September 11, 2001, attacks demonstrated the willingness of terrorists to inflict mass casualties on the United States. The anthrax attacks showed that "the terrorist use of biological weapons is no longer theoretical," according to arms control expert Jonathan B. Tucker. Whether or not America might be victimized again through the use of biological agents is a troubling question. CIA director George J. Tenet, testifying in Congress in February 2002, reported that his agency had proof that al-Qaeda, the terrorist network believed to be responsible for the September 11, 2001, attacks had been "pursuing a sophisticated biological weapons research program" in Afghanistan. In this chapter experts debate the possibility that biological weapons may be used again, with perhaps even deadlier consequences than in 2001.

*"This biological genie may pose a far
greater threat than 1,000 atomic bombs."*

Biological Agents Can Be Made into Weapons of Mass Destruction

Scott P. Layne and Michael H. Sommer

In the following viewpoint, written when Americans were debating military action against Iraq and its leader Saddam Hussein, Scott P. Layne and Michael H. Sommer raise the sobering possibility that biological weapons (which could possibly be used by Iraq in retaliation to U.S. military action) have the potential to infect and kill half the world's population. Such a nightmare scenario must be taken seriously, they argue, given recent advances in bioengineering research. In addition to being deadly, biological weapons have the advantage of being much cheaper to produce than chemical and nuclear weapons. Scott P. Layne is an associate professor of epidemiology at the University of California-Los Angeles (UCLA) School of Public Health. Michael H. Sommer is a visiting scholar at the Institute of Governmental Studies at the University of California at Berkeley.

As you read, consider the following questions:

1. What is the "bio-Armageddon scenario," according to Layne and Sommer?
2. What examples of biological research do the authors believe show how easy it has become to create biological weapons?
3. What two actions do Layne and Sommer recommend to deal with the threat of bioterrorism?

Scott P. Layne and Michael H. Sommer, "A Virus-Fed Doomsday," *Los Angeles Times*, October 10, 2002. Copyright © 2002 by the *Los Angeles Times*. Reproduced by permission.

The debate [in 2002] among the nation's politicians and the advice they're receiving from intelligence experts should not focus exclusively on diplomacy versus preemptive military action against [Iraqi dictator] Saddam Hussein. Instead, there is one nightmarish outcome—the so-called bio-Armageddon scenario—that is of immediate concern.

It goes like this: We go in to take out Hussein, and his obedient henchmen pull a "doomsday" switch, releasing contagious biological agents for which there is no vaccine and no cure. Not only are hundreds of thousands of American troops wiped out but, if Hussein wishes to die a martyr's death, the virulent agents are released to spread around the world and wipe out half of mankind.

Even mentioning this subject may seem like scaremongering, but it's not. In today's dicey world, this horrific possibility is a biological, military and political fact of life—or death—that cannot be dismissed out of hand.

How seriously has the bio-Armageddon scenario been weighed in councils of war? An Oct. 7 [2002] letter from CIA Director George Tenet to Senator Bob Graham (D-Fla.), chairman of the Intelligence Committee, stated that a cornered Hussein might use "his last chance to exact vengeance by taking a large number of victims with him."

It costs about $1 million to kill one person with a nuclear weapon, about $1,000 to kill one person with a chemical weapon and about $1 to kill one person with a biological weapon. Low cost alone may dictate that current and future terrorists will opt for the $1 biological killers.

Advances in Bioengineering

In 2001, a bombshell of a scientific paper, published in the *Journal of Virology*, revealed that a bioengineered form of mousepox—a close cousin of smallpox—was vaccine-resistant and 100% lethal. It showed that simply inserting one immune-inhibiting gene into mousepox was all it took.

Is it conceivable that Hussein's well-trained scientists, who crave to please their boss at any cost, have not read this paper and applied its findings to smallpox?

In 2002, another stunning paper in the research journal *Science* described the complete synthesis of the poliovirus genome in the test tube. This feat of bioengineering pointed out that deadly viruses, such as smallpox, can be resurrected in the test tube. No seed germs are required, as previously thought, just genetic sequences, training in molecular biology at the master's-in-science level and a few years of laboratory work.

Black Biology

Beyond the smallpox scenario, what has people worried is the impact of modern biotechnology. For better or worse, the world is in the midst of a stunning revolution in the life sciences. Scientists have already determined the complete genomic sequences for more than 30 microbes and even more viruses. The DNA code for the cholera pathogen (*Vibrio cholerae*) was recently published, and the genomes of more than 100 other microorganisms are now being sequenced—including the bacteria that cause anthrax, plague, dysentery and typhoid. Of course, the new information is critical for answering fundamental and practical questions in biology and medicine, and will be put to direct, practical use in a myriad of health-related applications. But what about "black biology"? Could biotechnology be used to produce a new generation of biowarfare agents with unprecedented power to destroy? Or is this just alarmist hype? No one can say for sure, but many molecular biologists familiar with the relevant technologies seem inclined to a pessimistic view.

A key reason for pessimism is the ease with which genetic manipulations are now accomplished. . . . Both bacteria and viruses may now be engineered to be qualitatively different from conventional bioweapon agents. In terms of bioweaponry, this includes imbuing them with such "desirable" attributes as safer handling, increased virulence, improved ability to target the host, greater difficulty of detection and easier distribution.

Steven M. Block, *American Scientist*, January 2001.

It's hard to underestimate or sugarcoat these scientific papers. They offer a blueprint for creating vaccine-resistant and highly lethal viruses that could, for example, render the current smallpox vaccine stockpile and the U.S. government's emergency vaccination program absolutely useless. This biological genie may pose a far greater threat than 1,000 atomic bombs.

It's no longer hypothetical to bioengineer such an agent. And less than $1 million would be required to create deadly and contagious agents.

In the wrong hands, a bioengineered virus could be bottled and used as an insurance policy against invasion and overthrow. And, if unleashed, it could change the very fabric of remaining modern civilization. At a minimum, too many people might be stricken to continue to operate oil refineries, power plants, airlines and communications.

New Policies Are Needed

A completely new appraisal and posture are needed to deal with these threats.

First, the U.S. needs to train and place more intelligence agents knowledgeable in this type of warfare throughout the world, because the work taking place in a secret offensive biological weapons program cannot be monitored from airplanes or satellites. It must be spied on firsthand.

Building our biological human intelligence capabilities will take years. It will require the scientific, law enforcement and national security communities to finally work together, which they have shown little inclination to do.

Second, we need to build a high-speed high-volume infectious disease laboratory and information processing system that links the molecular fingerprints of biological agents to their sources worldwide.

Such a system would provide comprehensive and rapid analyses of biological agents and, when every moment counts, it could help to save countless lives after an attack—both at home and abroad.

If we had such a laboratory and biological sample collection program working, we could test for the combined signatures of pox viruses and virus-altering proteins. If, for example, the two were found to reside in the wrong hands or places, we could take preemptive actions.

Here's the bottom line: Bio-Armageddon and biological blackmail cannot continue to remain as realistic options for terrorists.

> *"The biological weapon that creates a runaway effect, killing huge numbers rapidly, so far exists only in science fiction and preposterous Hollywood thrillers."*

Biological Agents Should Not Be Considered Weapons of Mass Destruction

Gregg Easterbrook

Gregg Easterbrook is a senior editor at the *New Republic* magazine and a visiting scholar at the Brookings Institution. In the following viewpoint, he questions the use of the term "weapons of mass destruction" to describe biological (and chemical) weapons. Although biological agents can be harmful to humans, they are difficult and impractical to use as weapons. Historic efforts to use biological weapons have resulted in very few fatalities, he notes, and concludes that the attention paid to biological weapons can distract Americans from a true weapon of mass destruction—the atomic bomb.

As you read, consider the following questions:

1. What is the public perception of biological weapons, according to Easterbrook?
2. Why is a mass outbreak of smallpox unlikely, in the author's view?
3. Why do bioweapons create greater public anxiety than they warrant, according to Easterbrook?

P oliticians, pundits, and the media . . . have used the phrase "weapons of mass destruction" as a constant shorthand for chemical, biological, and atomic arms. As of this writing [in September 2002], the phrase "weapons of mass destruction" had appeared in *The New York Times* in some 250 articles over the past month alone. And while I do not claim to have examined all of these citations, it is a safe bet that most referred collectively to chemical, biological, and atomic arms, implying equivalent power to inflict "death on a massive scale."

Yet their lethal potential is emphatically not equivalent. Chemical weapons are dangerous, to be sure, but not "weapons of mass destruction" in any meaningful sense. In actual use, chemical arms have proven *less* deadly than regular bombs, bullets, and artillery shells. . . .

Similarly, biological weapons are widely viewed with dread, though in actual use they have rarely done great harm. The most successful biological warfare to date took place nearly 250 years ago, when the British gave smallpox-laden blankets to French-affiliated Native Americans during the Seven Years' War. Japanese attempts to use biological weapons against China during World War II were of limited success. More recently there have been accidental releases of smallpox and anthrax in the Soviet Union and Ebola exposure in the United States; all did far less harm than would have been caused by the detonation of a single conventional bomb.

Biological agents are surely dangerous: Being alive, they can propagate, in theory "manufacturing" more of themselves from tiny initial amounts. But the biological weapon that creates a runaway effect, killing huge numbers rapidly, so far exists only in science fiction and preposterous Hollywood thrillers such as *Outbreak*. The living things of Earth have spent millions of years evolving defenses against runaway pathogens, and these defenses have grown stronger during the postwar era as public health has improved spectacularly in most nations. Deliberate, systematic distribution of weapons-grade anthrax in the United States in 2001 killed five people—terrible, but hardly "mass destruction" compared to the jet-fuel explosions that killed 3,000 on September 11, 2001, and the conventional bomb that killed 168 in Oklahoma City in 1995. Because actual attempts to use bioweapons have been few, it's hard to be sure; but it may well be that, like chemical weapons, biological agents will prove less dangerous than conventional arms, as well as more difficult for armies or terrorists to use.

Then there are atomic and nuclear devices—utterly, unmistakably "weapons of mass destruction." Pound for pound, these are the most awful constructions of human enterprise, thousands or millions of times more dangerous than any chemical or biological arms.

The phrase "weapons of mass destruction," then, obscures more than it clarifies. It lumps together a category of truly terrible weapons (atomic bombs) with two other categories that are either less dangerous than conventional weapons (chemical arms) or largely an unknown quantity (biological agents). . . .

Perception vs. Reality

Supposedly . . . [biological] weapons kill very rapidly in huge numbers. William Cohen, when secretary of defense under Bill Clinton, once held up a small bag of sugar and declared that an equivalent amount of anthrax spores could kill half the population of the District of Columbia. "Dark Winter," a bioterrorism war game conducted a few months before September 11, 2001, at Andrews Air Force Base—and featuring Sam Nunn as "President Nunn"—posited that a handful of terrorists with small quantities of smallpox could set in motion unstoppable events that would kill up to one million Americans. National newscasts have illustrated reports about biological weapons with video clips from the movie *Outbreak*, in which U.S. bombers obliterate entire areas, killing everyone within in order to halt a super-plague. Richard Preston's sci-fi thriller *The Cobra Event* depicted a biological weapon capable of killing everyone in New York City in 24 hours. Since Preston had previously written a more-or-less nonfiction best-seller, *The Hot Zone*, which claimed Ebola could kill millions unstoppably, his *Cobra Event* was said to have deeply disturbed President Clinton—even though *it was a sci-fi novel*. In 2002 the BBC aired a docudrama, which to the viewer looked awfully like a straight news show, in which a single terrorist with smallpox causes a global epidemic that kills 60 million people.

That is the public perception of biological weapons. Here is what has happened in actual use: In 1971 smallpox from the old Soviet bioweapons program got loose in Aralsk, Kazakhstan, a place with terribly low public health standards—life expectancy for men at birth was just 40 years. Despite these seemingly ideal conditions for a runaway plague, the smallpox killed a total of three people. In 1979 an explosion at a Soviet bioweapons plant near Sverdlovsk (now called Ekaterinburg), also a place with poor public health, released a large quantity of weapons-grade anthrax spores into the air. The anthrax killed 68 people. In 1989, monkeys carrying the Ebola virus were accidentally shipped to a government facility in Reston, Virginia, just outside Washington. Workers at the facility were exposed to the virus and then moved freely among friends and family for several days before the situation was discovered. This event—the subject of Preston's book *The Hot Zone*—has since been discussed as if it showed how vulnerable the United States is to bioterrorism. Usually skipped over in such discussions, however, is that the Ebola loosed near the nation's capital in 1989 did not cause a single death.

Historic efforts at killing large populations through biological warfare have met with mixed results. During World War II, Japanese army researchers bred fleas infected with bubonic plague, which were dropped in clouds over Chinese cities and dumped into Chinese water wells. This biological attack, directed against an impoverished population with almost no modern health care, is thought to have killed several thousand Chinese civilians; it was halted when the Japanese realized that plague-infected drinking water was killing their own soldiers in China. But conventional Japanese bombing of Chinese cities also killed thousands. Farther back, during medieval times, siege armies used catapults to hurl the bodies of bubonic-plague victims into cities, hoping to spread contagion. And that's about it for the actual use of biological weapons.

Public Health Defenses

Note that bioweapons have done steadily less harm in recent times, as public health infrastructure has improved. When the Aralsk smallpox outbreak happened, for example, Soviet officials moved rapidly to vaccinate the 50,000 people closest to the area; this stopped the disease, giving it no vulnerable hosts to jump to. Ebola had no impact in the United States in 1989, and anthrax had relatively little impact in 2001, because the releases occurred in areas of high public health and excellent health care services; the pathogens were rapidly isolated and antibiotics were given. In a world of ever-better public health (in the West, at least), using a bioweapon is like shooting a gun at someone wearing a bulletproof vest—the bullet is still dangerous, but there is a reasonable chance it will bounce off.

The Limits of Bioengineering

Some developments in biology have nightmarish potential. But many experts say that at present the reality of the threat posed by bioengineered [genetically engineered] weapons is probably much less than that from conventional [naturally occurring] biological agents. "The worst that you can imagine is probably not a very realistic scenario," says Albert Osterhaus, a virologist at Rotterdam University in the Netherlands. One reason for optimism is that pathogens engineered in the lab may struggle to survive, or quickly lose their imbued characteristics, if they were ever released. Evolution, argues [disease expert Paul] Ewald, is on our side. "People don't think about natural selection. If they did, they would have a clearer idea of what the dangers would be."

Because evolution is all about trade-offs between the costs and the benefits of different traits in particular environments, Ewald suspects that it would be extremely difficult to engineer all of the desired 'attributes' into a bioweapon and still have an organism that is transmitted effectively and predictably. In naturally occurring pathogens, he points out, traits such as virulence and transmissibility often counteract one another.

Carina Dennis, *Nature*, May 17, 2001.

Consider public health defenses against smallpox: American and European populations retain at least some residual smallpox immunity from the vaccinations that stopped about three decades ago. Estimates vary, but somewhere around half of the United States public probably has some resistance to smallpox, which would instill a partial "herd immunity" against outbreak—the disease could less easily jump from host to host. Smallpox must be spread by person-to-person contact; it does not waft on the breeze. This means that physically isolating an outbreak area (as was done at Aralsk) stops the spread of the disease. Vaccination as many as four days after exposure usually prevents death, as smallpox's incubation time is at least ten days. There are about 155 million doses of smallpox vaccine on hand in the United States—more than enough for all those who were never inoculated—and the government will have roughly twice that amount by the end of 2002. The reintroduction into society of smallpox, declared eradicated by the World Health Organization in 1980, would be a terrible thing. But would "mass destruction" result? Again, possible but not likely.

What's more, it is unclear that anyone other than the United States, Russia, and the World Health Organization has smallpox samples; the disease no longer exists in nature. Assuming terrorists did acquire some, smallpox would hardly be easy to distribute—aerosol forms last only for a short period and travel a short range, while person-to-person infection would be slowed by "herd immunity."

Anthrax, by contrast, can be spread as a long-lived aerosol, and Iraq is known to have cultured significant amounts of this bioweapon. Israel is relatively safe from an Iraqi anthrax attack, however, because anthrax probably cannot be delivered by missile: Anthrax-loaded warheads, arriving at hundreds of miles per hour, would immolate their own contents. Anthrax could be spread from a low-flying plane, or through the ventilation systems of large buildings. But a low-flying plane could drop bombs, too, and buildings could be blown up; moreover, conventional attacks of this nature would kill people right away, whereas bioweapon attacks would leave time for physicians to save the victims.

Other pathogens might also serve as bioweapons; foes could even employ genetically engineered crop blights designed not to kill people but to cause agricultural failures, the National Research Council warned. In theory the germs could be made more cheaply than bombs, putting them within the financial reach of terrorists; in theory they could be produced in small laboratories that are hard to target in counterstrikes; in theory they could even be carried to the target in someone's pocket. But that's all true only in theory. Actual experience suggests that biological weapons are both hard to make and hard to use, for many of the same reasons that medicines are hard to make and don't work unless administered precisely. Aum Shinrikyo [a Japanese cult] employed skilled scientists and spent freely to make "high-grade" anthrax, which it spread around Tokyo on several occasions. The cult gave up on anthrax after it failed to infect even a single person.

Why do bioweapons elicit such anxiety when recent experience suggests they pose less threat than bombs and bullets? Like chemical agents, bioweapons are invisible; human nature dictates that we fear what we cannot see. The American public also shows little understanding of the basics of public health, having developed a media-encouraged phobic conviction that minute quantities of laboratory-made substances are far more dangerous than everyday lifestyle risks. People imagine that one part per quadrillion of dioxin or the incredibly weak electromagnetic fields made by power lines are shocking health threats—yet they cheerfully consume vast amounts of fats and sugars despite the fact that obesity is the number-two cause of death in the United States.

One True Weapon of Mass Destruction

That leaves the one true "weapon of mass destruction" that Iraq or a terrorist might obtain: the atomic bomb.

There is nothing speculative or uncertain about the doomsday power of atomic bombs like those used at Hiroshima and Nagasaki, Japan, during World War II. (Its still more destructive sibling, the nuclear fusion bomb, is considered too complex for rogue states or terrorists to build.) At least 70,000 people died at Hiroshima, at least 40,000 at Nagasaki. A crude atomic bomb of similar power detonated in a modern city, where large skyscrapers would topple, could produce an even greater death toll. Unlike chemical weapons, there are no questions about whether the wind will blow away the agent or the sun dissolve it; horror is 100 percent certain. Unlike biological weapons, there is no exposure followed by gradual sickening during which doctors could labor to save most victims; horror is instant and irreversible. Everything about the atomic bomb is horrific and *known to work*.

Yet in debates about Iraq, and about global terrorism, everything that isn't a bullet or shell is lumped together under the rubric of "weapons of mass destruction." Virtually every national leader and most major publications invoke this phrase without seeming to care what it means; protests have come only from such quarters as Slate.com, *The Village Voice*, *Reason*, and *The Journal of Strategic Studies*. Endlessly referring to "weapons of mass destruction" in this way distracts us from focusing on the one weapon we can be certain causes mass destruction: the atomic bomb.

> "*Rapid developments in biotechnology . . .*
> *are unwittingly providing rogue groups*
> *and nations with inexpensive tools to*
> *fashion new and more potent bioweapons.*"

Biological Weapons Pose a Serious Danger to Americans

Tara O'Toole and Donald A. Henderson

In the following viewpoint, biological weapons experts Tara O'Toole and Donald A. Henderson assess the threat of bioterrorism. They contend that rogue nations or terrorist groups could use biological weapons to kill thousands or millions of people, making such weapons as potentially devastating as nuclear bombs. Unfortunately, the authors argue, the United States is at present ill-equipped to deal with a biological attack. The United States should strengthen controls on biological weapons research while preparing for a possible biological attack, they conclude. O'Toole directs the Center for Civilian Biodefense Strategies at Johns Hopkins University in Maryland. Henderson, a founder of the center and former dean of the Johns Hopkins School of Public Health, has served as a senior science adviser to the federal government on biological warfare issues.

As you read, consider the following questions:
1. How many countries do O'Toole and Henderson believe are working on biological weapons?
2. Why might an outbreak of smallpox be catastrophic, according to the authors?

Tara O'Toole and Donald A. Henderson, "A Clearly Present Danger," *Harvard International Review*, vol. 23, Fall 2001, pp. 49–53. Copyright © 2001 by *Harvard International Review*. Reproduced by permission.

S erious concerns about the possible use of microbes as weapons of terror have heightened markedly over the past five years. This threat, mysterious and little understood, has spawned a spate of docudramas, books, and speculative scenarios, each conjuring up scarcely believable epidemic disasters. Although many such stories are best characterized as flights of science fiction, it has nonetheless become increasingly apparent that the occurrence of a bioterrorist event is entirely plausible and could be catastrophic. All countries are at risk. Instruction on how to prepare effective weapons is now available on the Internet, as are offers by laboratories in various parts of the world to provide strains of some of the most deadly microbes. Rapid developments in biotechnology are opening new vistas in medicine, but, at the same time, they are unwittingly providing rogue groups and nations with inexpensive tools to fashion new and more potent bioweapons. Meanwhile, during the past decade, large numbers of Russian scientists have left the extensive biological-weapons complex of the former Soviet Union and have been actively recruited for work in other countries. Thirty years ago, there were only four countries known to be working with biological weapons. Now, however, there are thought to be as many as 12 to 14.

Assessing the Threat

The United States ended its offensive bioweapons program in 1970. Like most countries, the United States has been slow to consider and implement possible defensive policies against "deliberate epidemics." Internationally, primary reliance has rested with the 1972 Biologic and Toxin Weapons Convention. This agreement had been signed by most countries but, as was discovered during the past decade, its terms were flagrantly violated both by Iraq and the former Soviet Union. Although the Convention mandates that no country undertake research on or production of biological weapons, there are no provisions or procedures for verification and enforcement. Countless meetings over a period of many years have so far failed to identify suitable mechanisms that countries could agree upon. . . .

A new perspective on the threat is provided by a 2001 report of the US Commission on National Security in the 21st century. It singles out bioweapons as perhaps the greatest threat that the United States might face in the next century. Admiral Stansfield Turner, former Director of the US Central Intelligence Agency, believes that, besides nuclear weapons, the only other weapon class with the capacity to bring the nation past the "point of non-recovery" is biological weapons. In 1993, the US Office of Technology Assessment illustrated this threat in their estimate that 100 grams of anthrax released upwind of a large American city—say Washington, DC—could cause between 130,000 and three million deaths, depending on weather and other variables. At the high end, this degree of carnage is of a magnitude comparable to that caused by a hydrogen bomb, far exceeding what a chemical weapon could do. There is no doubt that biological weapons can be effective, and their utility has been demonstrated by all possible means short of war.

Nations and Groups Interested in Bioterrorism

Heightened interest in bioterrorism by a number of nations can be attributed in significant part to the massive research and development program in this field conducted by the former Soviet Union. In the early 1990s, the West first learned from high-level Soviet defectors that in 1972, when other countries were ending their programs, the Soviet Union opted to expand and modernize its biological-weapons program and to begin to develop genetically engineered pathogens that could serve as weapons. Biopreparat, an ostensibly civilian operation, recruited outstanding scientists from throughout the country; at its peak, it employed over 30,000 people. Another 15,000 scientists were employed in a special military program, and 10,000 more were in an agricultural program intended to devise organisms to attack crops. Besides major research and development efforts, Biopreparat's agenda included the manipulation of microbes so that they could survive delivery on missile warheads, the manufacture of tons of dried anthrax spores and a number of other agents, and the establishment of an industrial capacity for the large-scale production of smallpox virus and antibiotic-resistant strains of plague. Much of the civilian component of this industrial complex is in the process of converting to other areas of research and to commercial production of biologics. However, the biological laboratories under military control remain closed to visitors. Iraq also acknowledges having developed a major program for research and production of biological weapons, primarily anthrax and botulinum toxin. This program remains intact, with its full complement of personnel.

It is generally agreed that overt use of a biological weapon by a nation-state is unlikely if for no other reason than fear of severe retribution were its role to be identified. However, because the production of biological weapons requires only a modest amount of readily procurable equipment, comparatively little space, and few personnel, it is a potential weapon for use by any of a number of extremist groups intent on inflicting large numbers of casualties. Two groups that have used or threatened to use biological weapons are the Osama bin Laden group and the Japanese religious cult, Aum Shinrikyo. The latter released sarin gas in the Tokyo subway in 1995 and had previously sought unsuccessfully to spread anthrax spores and botulinum toxin throughout metropolitan Tokyo.

Concern about the possible consequences of the prodigious advances now occurring in the biosciences was recently expressed by Harvard University Professor Matthew Meselson: "Every major technology—metallurgy, explosives, internal combustion, aviation, electronics, nuclear energy—has been extensively exploited, not only for peaceful purposes, but also for hostile ones. Any major turn to the use of biotechnology for hostile purposes could have consequences qualitatively very different from those that have followed from the hostile exploitation of earlier technologies. Unlike . . . conventional or even nuclear weapons, biotechnology has the potential to place mass destructive capability in a multitude of hands."

The Effects of an Attack

The consequence of a biological weapons attack would be an epidemic, the nature of which would depend on the organism used. In theory, virtually any infectious microbe could be considered a candidate for use as a weapon, but some diseases have more serious consequences than others. For example, cities have continued to function essentially normally even in the face of community-wide epidemics of influenza. Conversely, in 1994, nearly half of the population of a large Indian city fled when only tens of cases of plague were reported. In 1999, an expert committee convened at Johns Hopkins University analyzed the various attributes of different diseases in terms of their capacity to cause a public-health emergency sufficiently serious as to compromise the functioning of government. Diseases considered to pose, by far, the most serious problems were smallpox, anthrax, plague, botulinum toxin, tularemia, and a group of agents such as Ebola virus that result in hemorrhagic disease. Any one of these organisms dispersed as a fine particle aerosol could result, under the right conditions, in thousands of casualties. Several of these organisms, as well as others, could also be dispersed in water or food to cause substantial numbers of infections.

The most serious bioterrorism scenarios would result from a covert, unannounced attack. There would be no explosion or other evidence of release—just the silent dispersion of an invisible, fine-particle aerosol without odor or taste. In all probability, the first knowledge that something had happened would occur when patients started appearing in the emergency rooms and in doctors' offices with strange illnesses, some severe and rapidly fatal. This could be days to weeks after the release. Some infected persons, by then, may have traveled to other countries and continents.

Even worse, physicians are not trained to diagnose the pathogens thought most likely to be used as bioweapons. Few have ever seen anthrax or smallpox or pneumonic plague, and ordinary hospital laboratories do not have the necessary reagents or experience to rapidly diagnose these infections.

Epidemics

Few persons have witnessed or endeavored to cope with a fast-moving lethal epidemic. Epidemics tend to be terrorizing. In 1994, cases of plague occurred in Surat, India, as a result of an ecological disruption caused by earthquakes. Within 12 hours of media reports of a deadly, mysterious fever, people began streaming out of the city. Among the first to leave were many from the medical community. Eventually half a million people fled, leaving the city a ghost town. It is estimated that India lost US$2 billion dollars in trade, embargoes, and industrial output. Some 6,500 illnesses and 56 deaths were reported to have occurred, although later studies indicate that few were actually plague cases—a disease, incidentally, that is treatable with antibiotics.

Bioterrorism Likely to Occur

It is my belief that a bioterrorism event, possibly one of even catastrophic proportions, is likely to occur in the United States within the next several years. This conclusion is based on the merging of 3 critical elements: terrorists with sufficient motivation and expertise, the availability of pathogens able to be effectively transmitted to large populations and cause serious disease, and the methods for dissemination of such agents.

Michael T. Osterholm, *American Journal of Infection Control*, December 1999.

A second characteristic of epidemics is that they have the potential to cause large numbers of casualties. The best known example of a pandemic (global epidemic) is the so-called swine influenza of 1918–1919. It circled the world in about four months in an era of cargo ships and railroads and trolley cars. In all, 20 to 40 million people died. The mortality rate, however, was "only" two percent. If it had had a mortality rate similar to that of a new influenza strain such as that discovered in Hong Kong three years ago, more than 15 times as many deaths would have occurred. Fortunately, the Hong Kong outbreak was contained before spreading abroad.

A third special problem posed by epidemics relates to difficulties associated with control of a contagious disease. In 1972, there was a smallpox outbreak in Yugoslavia when a returning pilgrim became ill shortly after returning home. He was met and honored by family and friends. Eleven of his contacts became ill two weeks later. The doctors who treated them did not suspect smallpox—no cases had occurred in Yugoslavia in 45 years, and compulsory vaccination against smallpox was still in practice. Another two weeks elapsed before the disease was correctly diagnosed. By that time, cases were occurring in many different towns and cities in different regions; 150 people were already sick or dying. To prevent spread of the disease, the surrounding countries closed their borders to trade and transport. Yugoslav authorities decided that their only option was to vaccinate the entire population and this they did—all 20 million people. Ten thousand patient contacts were isolated in hotels and apartment buildings until after the incubation period had passed. As a result of such heroic efforts, the epidemic was contained. It is worth bearing in mind that, compared to other outbreaks, this was not a large epidemic—it only led to 175 cases with 35 deaths.

Smallpox

An outbreak of smallpox today could be catastrophic. Vaccination ceased in the United States in 1972 and, by 1980, throughout the world. Thus, half or more of the population is fully susceptible to the disease, as are many of those who were vaccinated before 1980, since vaccination immunity decreases over time. The disease spreads from person to person and, because so few are now protected, each patient would probably infect 10 to 20 others if an epidemic were to occur today. Thus, every 10 to 14 days, there would be a new wave of patients that, if uncontrolled, would be at least an order of magnitude larger than the previous one. There is no treatment; 30 percent of patients die. The only effective measures that could be taken would be vaccination and isolation of patients so they could not spread the disease. Vaccination protects within about seven to eight days after administration. In an epidemic, efforts are made to immediately vaccinate all persons who have been in contact with patients since they first became ill—in the hospitals where patients are housed as well as contacts in the family, school and work place.

But there is an even larger problem. The only available vaccine was made and stored before 1980, and while some of it remains potent today, there is very little available. There are no manufacturers anywhere in the world today. Although the US Centers for Disease Control and Prevention (CDC) have recently negotiated a contract to produce 40 million doses of smallpox vaccine, the first product will not be ready until 2004. If an outbreak of as few as 50 patients were to occur, demands for vaccine supplies would exhaust the limited available stocks within four to six weeks.

The Public Health Response

Effective management of an epidemic is a complex and difficult task, often compounded by high levels of public anxiety and even, on occasion, panic. Presently, there is little experience upon which to build management skills. Large-scale epidemics with high death rates are now uncommon in most parts of the world, and there are few, if any, who have had experience with any of the diseases identified as potentially the most dangerous biological weapons. The last smallpox epidemics occurred more than 25 years ago and the details of the only known epidemic of inhalation anthrax—which resulted from a 1979 accidental release of anthrax spores from a Soviet bioweapons plant—are incomplete.

The medical and public health infrastructures in most countries are marginal at best and nonexistent at worst. Hospitals today are usually full to overflowing and have little capacity to deal with even a small, sudden surge of patients. Few would be able to prevent in-hospital disease transmission, and most are short of staff for almost every important task. The public health infrastructure in most parts of the world has been steadily eroding over several decades as principal investments have been directed to tertiary curative care facilities and therapeutic drugs.

Surveillance to detect disease outbreaks is seriously deficient everywhere, including in the United States, primarily because of the lack of public health expertise. Those who know well the status of public health in the United States suspect that New York's West Nile encephalitis outbreak would probably have gone undetected in 90 percent of US cities and without preventive measures until so late in the autumn as to be of no value. Internationally, surveillance is even poorer. Who knows how many other new or emergent infections as serious as AIDS are now spreading through remote villages of Africa or Asia?

In efforts to cut costs, pharmaceutical firms have reduced inventories of both antibiotics and vaccines with the result that shortages of both are occurring regularly. Thus, absent

41

special measures being taken, there would be no way to deal with an epidemic such as plague or anthrax that required a surge in use of antibiotics. A fundamental problem is that public health and medical-care systems are poorly equipped today to deal with any sudden surge of cases, whether naturally occurring or propagated by a terrorist. Any emergency large-scale vaccination or drug-distribution program would far exceed the capacity of most public health departments. This is especially true in the developing world where, even today, simple programs to provide daily doses of drugs to treat a growing tuberculosis epidemic, for example, are beyond the capacity of most health systems.

What Can Be Done

Perhaps the most important principle to be recognized is that for nearly a generation, we have become increasingly complacent about the threat of the ever-changing, ever-mutating microbial world. However, as Nobel Prize laureate Joshua Lederberg has pointed out, viruses and bacteria are man's only serious competitors for dominion of the planet—and the ultimate outcome is by no means a foregone conclusion. A grim scenario, for example, would be an epidemic of an HIV/AIDS-like virus that spreads as rapidly as influenza but does not produce serious symptoms for many years. How prepared would we be to detect, diagnose, and deal with such an occurrence with either drugs or vaccines? Epidemics, whether occurring naturally or as a result of deliberate release, are serious threats to the well-being of peoples everywhere. There are serious penalties to be paid by the unprepared.

Consideration must be given to the development of an international surveillance network of epidemiologists and laboratories, prepared to quickly investigate and determine the cause of disease epidemics wherever they might occur. Disease epidemics in the modern world are more than national problems; they are potentially threats to international security. The essential component of disease surveillance for infectious diseases at a local level is that clinicians treating patients in emergency rooms or health centers accustom themselves to contacting public health officials immediately whenever they encounter suspiciously severe cases of common illness or an unusual cluster of cases. This will undoubtedly require an expansion of public health capacities, but it is a small price to pay for the possible prevention of a catastrophe.

Prevention of bioterrorism, to the extent that this is possible, should be a high priority. It is imperative to build a universal consensus, particularly among scientists, that the development, production, or dissemination of biological weapons by any persons, laboratories, or governments would be regarded by the world community as one of the most serious of all crimes. Strengthening the Biological and Toxin Weapons Convention to provide for some means for verification of compliance is also desirable, but it is unlikely to be sufficient. Plans and preparations for dealing with outbreaks of severe disease and other catastrophes involving large numbers of casualties should be a basic responsibility of national and local governments in all countries. . . .

The good news is that some active discussion is already beginning to take place. The bad news is that this discussion is a modern tower of Babel, with many groups talking at the same time, each with different objectives that are incomprehensible to others. The world at large is only beginning to recognize that bioterrorism is a threat equivalent to, and perhaps greater than, the threat of nuclear weapons. We are only now becoming familiar with a threat that will be with us for many years to come.

"We need to find ways to manage the normal feelings of anxiety and vulnerability that result . . . from fear of terrorism."

Americans Should Not Be Overly Worried About Biological Weapons

Henry I. Miller and Sherri Ferris

Henry I. Miller is a research fellow at the Hoover Institution; his works include the book *To America's Health: A Proposal to Reform the Food and Drug Administration*. Sherri Ferris is a marriage and family therapist. In the following viewpoint, written during the 2002 anthrax crisis when five people died after opening letters contaminated with this agent, Miller and Ferris argue that public anxiety about biological terrorism causes stress and is itself a problem that must be addressed. Miller and Ferris argue that the media has caused unnecessary panic by exaggerating the threat posed by bioterrorism. They contend that doomsday scenarios involving biological weapons will most likely never come to pass, and urge Americans to manage their fears about biological weapons.

As you read, consider the following questions:
1. What evidence do Miller and Ferris cite to support their contention that American public anxiety is increasing?
2. What factors make a biological attack using the smallpox virus unlikely to succeed in creating a mass epidemic, according to the authors?

Henry I. Miller and Sherri Ferris, "The New Normalcy," *Hoover Digest*, Winter 2002, pp. 104–14. Copyright © 2002 by *Hoover Digest*. Reproduced by permission.

Americans are feeling anxious, edgy, and vulnerable—with good reason. The appearance of cases of anthrax [in September and October 2001], innumerable hoaxes and false alarms about terrorist attacks, the specter of terrorists using smallpox, combined with the contraction of the U.S. economy and spiraling unemployment, have disrupted our lives. And the mixed messages we've gotten from officials—be vigilant but return to your routines; we have no idea about the source of the anthrax, but everything is under control—are little help.

Many people report emotional instability, difficulty sleeping and concentrating, and unease about various activities, including entering tall buildings, traveling, and opening mail. Some in the most affected regions of the country are increasingly resorting to antianxiety drugs; prescriptions for these medications have risen sharply in New York and Washington, D.C. [where the September 11, 2001, terrorist attacks occurred.] According to NDC-Health, a company that collects data for the health care industry, the number of new prescriptions for alprazolam (the generic version of Xanax) was 22 percent greater in the Washington area and 12 percent greater in New York during the week ending September 28 [2002], compared to a year earlier (nationally, these prescriptions were up 6.3 percent). Prescriptions for diazepam (the generic version of Valium) increased 14 percent in Washington and 8 percent in New York, compared to the same week last year (nationally, the increase was 3 percent).

Our individual angst is likely to get worse before it gets better. President George W. Bush, Secretary of Defense Donald Rumsfeld, and other government officials have reminded us repeatedly that there will be no quick, definitive victory against this adversary, no D-Day invasion, no signing of a peace treaty on the deck of a battleship. More acts of terror against American civilians—adulteration of foods, Oklahoma City–style bombs, or other means—would not be surprising. And these could emanate not only from foreign terrorists but from homegrown crazies who have personality disorders, bear grudges, or are seeking their 15 minutes of fame.

The Media Stoke Fears

The media have only added to the frenzy of fear. Months before the September 11 [2001] attacks, Tad Friend wrote in the *New Yorker* that "it often seems that there is only one show on television, 'Dateline NBC: 48 Hours of 20/20, PrimeTime Thursday,' and that this show endlessly repeats one basic story: The Thing That Went Terribly Wrong." Well, now that something *has* gone terribly wrong, the networks—especially the cable news networks—are desperate to fill the broadcast day with accounts of the endless, continuous, relentless—and often inaccurate—details. For example, Detroit television station WXYZ-TV aired a report questioning the security of the laboratory of University of Michigan pathologist James R. Baker, inaccurately identified as an "anthrax researcher." (He has, however, worked in the past with the harmless related bacterium *Bacillus cereus*, which is used to make food additives and medicines.) When the TV crew attempted to enter Baker's laboratory, they were blocked by a locked door and, later, challenged by lab personnel. But scenes of the reporter freely entering an adjacent laboratory, even though it is used to study *hearing*, left the impression that university labs were vulnerable. The video, which aired several times over two days, forced university public relations officials to work frantically to calm public fears about campus security.

We must, as a nation, undertake various measures to prevent, prepare, and respond to bioterrorism. . . . There are also things that we, as individuals, can do to manage and reduce anxiety while remaining appropriately vigilant. This is important because hypervigilance and sustained anxiety cause stress—which predisposes us to infections, gastritis, ulcers, headache, and suicide—and lower productivity.

The idea of biological warfare, which boasts a long and sordid history, elicits the kind of images that writer George Orwell called "vague fears and horrible imaginings." It involves organisms that cause illnesses like "the black death," or bubonic plague, which is caused by the bacterium *Yersinia pestis*. In the fourteenth century, an army besieging Kaffa, a Russian Black Sea port, catapulted plague-infected corpses over the city walls. In the eighteenth century, at the end of the French and Indian Wars (1754–63), British soldiers distributed blankets that had been used by smallpox patients to American Indians and caused a devastating epidemic. Japan used plague and other bacteria against China in the 1930s and 1940s. And in 1984 more than 750 people suffered food poisoning in Oregon after members of a cult, attempting to disrupt the results of a local election, spread salmonella bacteria on salad bars in four restaurants.

Although bacteria and other microorganisms can sicken or even kill an individual, their ability to spread and cause "secondary" cases—infection of household or community contacts—is often limited. A worldwide threat from an "Andromeda strain" is largely the stuff of science fiction for a sound biological reason: Bacteria and viruses need living hosts to provide shelter and sustenance if they are to survive and thrive and therefore cannot kill those hosts too quickly or too often.

Unintentional Experiments

During the past half century, university and government laboratories working with infectious agents that cause diseases such as anthrax and bubonic plague have unintentionally performed what amounts to small-scale biological warfare "experiments"—in other words, laboratory accidents in which organisms were released.

The outcomes of these incidents are revealing. The U.S. Centers for Disease Control in Atlanta, which tracks such incidents in its own laboratories, recorded 109 laboratory-associated infections during the period 1947–73 but not a single secondary case. The National Animal Disease Center reported a similar experience, with no secondary cases occurring in either laboratory or nonlaboratory contacts of 18 laboratory-associated cases during the period 1960–75.

The medical literature similarly reveals only a handful of persons secondarily infected. In 1948–50, six cases of Q fever (a disease caused by intracellular parasites called *Rickettsia*) were reported in employees of a commercial laundry that handled linens and uniforms from a laboratory that conducted research with the agent; one case of Q fever in a visitor to a laboratory; and two cases of Q fever in household contacts of a laboratory scientist. A secondary case of a disease caused by an Ebola-like virus in the wife of a primary case was presumed to have been transmitted sexually two months after the husband's discharge from the hospital in 1967. One case of Monkey B virus transmission from an infected animal care technician to his wife apparently resulted from contact of the virus with a break in her skin. Finally, three secondary cases of smallpox were reported in two laboratory-associated outbreaks in England in 1973 and 1978.

Sack. © 2001 by Tribune Information Services. Reprinted with permission.

The occurrence of anthrax, caused by the bacterium *Bacillus anthracis*, in industrial settings is also instructive. Historically, workers involved with certain animal products were at highest risk, but truly 18 cases of inhalational (lung-introduced) anthrax were reported in the United States from 1900 to 1978, with the majority occurring in goatskin, wool, or tannery workers. Human-to-human transmission of anthrax has never been reported. Thus, anthrax is not contagious in the manner of some viruses such as influenza and rhinoviruses (which cause most common colds) or tuberculosis, which is caused by the bacterium *Mycobacterium tuberculosis*.

Facts About Smallpox

Considered solely from the medical and epidemiological vantage points, smallpox is probably the most feared and potentially devastating of all infectious agents. Smallpox spreads from person to person, primarily via droplets or aerosols expelled from the throat of infected persons, by direct contact, and via contaminated clothing and bed linens. It is fatal in perhaps a third of previously unvaccinated victims. However, the likelihood of smallpox virus being used by terrorists is considered very low; and even were it to occur, techniques and technology (that is, stockpiled vaccine) are available to prevent an epidemic. The following are relevant facts:

• Smallpox virus no longer occurs in nature but is limited to two legitimate repositories, one in the United States, the other in Russia (and perhaps illegitimately in a very small number of other countries). It is, therefore, very difficult to obtain, and also to cultivate and disseminate.

• Smallpox is not immediately contagious. It becomes contagious only after an incubation period and appearance of the characteristic rash, by which time the victim is prostrate, bedridden, and probably hospitalized. Therefore, the scenario in which a terrorist infects himself and spreads the disease widely through the population is not realistic.

• Although smallpox vaccination in the United States ended in 1972, individuals who were vaccinated before that time retain significant immunity from these immunizations, both against contracting smallpox and against a fatal outcome in case of infection.

• Public health authorities have at their disposal various proven epidemiologic and medical interventions. Early detection, quarantine of infected individuals, identification of contacts, and focused, aggressive vaccination—an approach dubbed "quarantine-ring vaccination"—are the essential elements of a control regime. Approximately 15 million doses of smallpox vaccine are now available in the United States, and data suggest that these could be diluted fivefold, to yield about 75 million doses. Federal officials have recently negotiated contracts to obtain approximately 150 million additional doses.

• The government has taken steps to cope with the possibility of a terrorist attack involving smallpox by educating doctors to recognize the disease and by vaccinating small teams of experts who can rush to any part of the country to contain and treat a suspected outbreak.

Preparing for the Unthinkable

What can we do to prevent and prepare for additional bioterrorism?

First, law enforcement, military, and intelligence agencies must expand their intelligence-gathering on nations and terrorist groups capable of launching attacks with biological agents.

Second, local police and paramedics should be trained to consider the possibility of biological weapons in incidents where large numbers of people suddenly become ill. Such incidents require behavior that is different from emergency workers' usual instincts: During conventional hostage situations and after explosions or earthquakes, the correct course is often to get as close to the incident as rapidly as possible; however, for biological or chemical exposures, it may be important for those responding initially to avoid becoming additional victims, either by donning appropriate protective gear or by medical prophylaxis and treatment.

Third, health care facilities must have emergency plans in place for sudden large numbers of contaminated or infected individuals. These plans must include rapid recognition of the incident, staff and facility protection, patient decontamination and triage, drug and other therapy, and coordination with external agencies. Practicing physicians and other health care workers should receive written reminders about the symptoms of infection with biological warfare agents; very few have seen—or been taught by someone who has seen—even a single case of anthrax, smallpox, or plague.

Finally, police departments and public health authorities need to formulate strategies for various contingencies, which should include stockpiled protective clothing, designated laboratories for rapid diagnosis, a procedure for notifying hospitals and transporting patients to them, and arrangements to obtain expert advice on short notice.

Much of what public health workers and institutions need to do to combat bioterrorism is similar to confronting natural disease outbreaks, such as Legionnaire's disease, influenza, and food poisoning. By far the greatest threat to individuals is not from criminal acts but from common naturally occurring infections, so everyone should be immunized against influenza and hepatitis A and B, and people over 55 (and those with any chronic disease) also should get the pneumococcus vaccine.

Living with Terrorism

This kind of vigilance and planning would reflect the admonition by Louis Pasteur, the father of bacteriology, that "chance favors only the prepared mind." But these societal measures are not in themselves sufficient. For one thing, government planners, intelligence operatives, law enforcement officers, and health professionals cannot do the entire job themselves. Individuals—civilians—are an important part of the solution. "Solution" may, however, not be the right word, because, as Stanford physicist and Hoover fellow Sidney Drell has said, "We're not going to solve the problem of terrorism; we're going to have to learn how to live with it." Indeed, many of us do, already, under certain circumstances. Americans in the military or diplomatic service who are posted to various bases and embassies around the world, as well as many employees of international companies, adapt and learn how to cope with their circumstances. What constitutes safe and appropriate behavior varies from place to place: Kiev is different from Khartoum, Rome from Ramallah.

Another way to think about the need to cope with new and increased threats to our well-being—especially the kinds of "low probability, high-impact" events represented by car bombs on bridges or attacks with bioterror agents—is that they are highly context-specific. In other words, we adjust our thresholds of concern according to what common sense and recent events tell us. If you were to cut an avocado in half and find a black bruise on the periphery, you'd probably simply cut away the blemish—unless there had been a recent rash of terrorists' injecting cyanide into fresh fruits and vegetables in supermarkets, in which case you might decide to discard the fruit.

Managing Our Fear

As Americans try to define collectively and individually what Vice President Dick Cheney has called the "new normalcy," we need to find ways to manage the normal feelings of anxiety and vulnerability that result not only from fear of terrorism directly, but from concerns about the slowing economy and increasing unemployment.

Franklin D. Roosevelt's observation that "the only thing we have to fear is fear itself" reflects that feelings of anxiety and vulnerability are normal in extraordinary times but that they can be debilitating to our lives, both individually and collectively. An important part of our moving forward to define the new normalcy will be to manage our fear.

"Its lethality and difficulty to cure make [anthrax] a potent bioweapon."

Anthrax Is a Serious Threat

Sallie Baliunas

In the fall of 2001 letters containing a white powder form of anthrax were mailed to political and media figures. Five people died and at least thirteen others were infected (the sender of the letters remained unknown at the end of 2002). Anthrax is a disease caused by a bacteria that exists naturally in livestock animals; it is nearly always fatal to humans if it is caught by inhalation and left untreated. In the following viewpoint, Sallie Baliunas describes the disease, its causes, and its symptoms. The hardiness and lethality of the anthrax bacterium has made it a prime candidate for biological warfare, she writes. In consequence, she argues, anthrax should be considered a serious threat to human health. Baliunas is an astrophysicist at the Harvard-Smithsonian Center for Astrophysics and a senior scientist at the George C. Marshall Institute in Washington, D.C.

As you read, consider the following questions:

1. What makes anthrax bacilli so durable, according to Baliunas?
2. What incident in the Soviet Union involving anthrax does the author describe?
3. What steps should America take to protect itself against anthrax, in Baliunas's view?

On June 8, 2001, President George W. Bush called for re-mediation of the threat of biological warfare because it is one of the "true threats of the 21st century." His words proved prescient, as by September [2001] this nation suffered the world's first bioattack of the 21st century with anthrax.

As investigators scratch for leads as to the source of strains of anthrax and the perpetrators of bioassaults taking the lives of people as divergent as a Florida reporter, Washington postal workers and a grandmother in Connecticut, they are dealing with a threat nearly as old as mankind. [No suspect had been arrested at the end of 2002.]

Anthrax as a weapon of terror may have roots reaching back to two plagues that visited Biblical Egypt. In *Exodus* Chapter 9, one of those plagues was described as a "very rare pestilence" on sheep, cattle, camels and oxen. For the next plague, Moses was directed to toss ashes on the wind, which "will become fine dust" that attacks both "man and beast" with boils and pustules. The stated rarity, association with grazing animals, dissemination by motes of dust or ashes and appearance of boils suggest anthrax, a bacterial disease.

The symptom of skin lesions described in *Exodus* may have been the less deadly cutaneous form of anthrax. It infects the body through the skin, one of three forms since identified by science for anthrax disease. Inhalation, or pulmonary, anthrax that enters through the lungs, is the cause of the six deaths in this country since [the September 11, 2001, terrorist attacks]. Its lethality and difficulty to cure make it a potent bioweapon.

Anthrax: Bacteria and Pathogen

The source for all anthrax infections is a common bacterium, *Bacillus anthracis*. Bacteria fall generally among one of three classes by shape: sphere (*coccus*), spiral (*spirillum*) and rod (*bacillus*). So, anthrax is rod shaped. It is relatively large as bacterial sizes go—as big as 2 by 10 microns, or roughly one by five ten-thousandths of an inch.

Not all bacteria are deadly. They often survive by living off host organisms, even benefiting their hosts. Of the rod-shaped species, many are harmless; in contrast, *anthracis* is lethal, especially when inhaled. And because it causes disease, that makes *anthracis* a pathogen.

Pathogens that kill their host often survive because they can move to other hosts as they come in contact with them. Spores need to invade directly each victim. Anthrax bacilli normally attack herbivores such as sheep, horses, goats and cattle, and when an infected animal dies, the bacilli escape the carcass to form spores that guard their genetic code or DNA with an exceptionally durable capsule. Effectively protected against deterioration in the environment, the spores of anthrax bacilli can persist decades. They can contaminate soil and infect new hosts, primarily the herbivores. Insects that feed on live infected animals or vultures that consume carcasses also can spread the spores.

But while anthrax is not contagious from person to person, its pulmonary form is particularly virulent. Once inhaled, spores move fast from the lungs to the lymph nodes near the heart and major blood vessels. The entering spores, viewed by the host as an invasion by a foreign body, trigger a counterattack by one of the human body's remarkable defense systems, the white blood cells. They ingest and attempt to digest the spores to destroy them. But encased in their protective coats, the tough spores may survive, and then scavenge metabolic material from the white blood cells in order to reproduce. Within a day or days, newly made anthrax bacilli burst from the white blood cells, hungering for more host cells and discharging toxins. Those toxins are extremely potent, destroying surrounding body tissue and rapidly overwhelming the host with blood poisoning, organ failure and death.

Getting It Under Control

Ironically, for all the devastation anthrax can sow, the study of anthrax itself led to a tremendous advance in conquering many horrific infectious diseases.

The great chemist Louis Pasteur in the mid-19th century founded the theory that microorganisms, or "germs," were microscopic agents of infectious disease. Other of Pasteur's great accomplishments include the development of the pasteurization process to keep milk supplies safe, discovery of the agent of silk worm disease, and creation of a vaccine successful in preventing hydrophobia, or rabies.

With germ theory gaining consideration as a cause of infectious disease, Robert Koch in 1876 proved that *bacillus anthracis* is the bacterium that produces anthrax. Pasteur then not only confirmed the bacillus as the germ responsible for anthrax, but also worked to reduce the bacteria to a less potent state. The weakened, or "attenuated," form of the bacillus was employed as a vaccine that, when injected into potential animal hosts, tries to stimulate the body's immune system to recognize and defend against a future invasion by the bacillus. The early anthrax vaccinations were of limited success, in part because of anthrax's virulence. Yet, astonishing success against other diseases derived from Pasteur's study of the technique of vaccination and germ theory.

Margulies. © 2001 by *The New Jersey Record*. Reprinted with permission.

Vaccination has vanquished many infectious diseases and so lengthened the human life span. But even as the anthrax vaccine to prevent infection has improved, it is not yet ready for widespread inoculation of the population. That leaves treatment after exposure, when antibiotics are given to attack the bacilli created in the host. Because the bacilli reproduce rapidly, antibiotic therapy must ideally begin just after exposure—often a fact difficult to assess. The race to kill the bacilli before they massively reproduce is crucial in surviving anthrax because of the toxin's lethality.

The Allure of Bioterror

The lethality—coupled with the hardiness and persistence—of bioterror agents such as anthrax . . . has prompted governments to fear for civilian safety and establish something of a breakwater against their widespread use.

President Abraham Lincoln, during the Civil War, was among the first leaders to direct troops to spare or protect civilians and civilian institutions when possible. His "General Orders 100" for Federal Troops became a building block for codes of conduct developed at international conferences at The Hague in the Netherlands in 1899 and 1907. Among atrocities prohibited by codes written there were the use of poison gas or other poison during warfare.

Yet, just as General William Tecumseh Sherman destroyed civilian property in his race to the sea during the Civil War, combatants in World War I, including the United States, used murderous chemical agents like chlorine, mustard gas or phosgene despite international pressure.

And subsequent agreements, such as the 1972 Biological and Toxin Weapons Convention, signed by almost every nation and forbidding developing or stockpiling biological agents for other than peaceful purposes, have not eliminated bio or chemical weapons as a threat.

The Soviet Union, despite signing the 1972 convention, appears to have disobeyed it with tragic consequences for their own people. Tantalized by its potential to provide a strategic advantage, the Soviets escalated bio-weapon development, leading in 1979 to the accidental release of anthrax from a lab in Yekaterinburg at Sverdlovsk. The plume of vapor released in that accident killed at least 66 people.

It was from that event that the incubation period for the disease was estimated to be as long as 43 days after exposure, leading to current prophylactic treatment by antibiotics for 60 days.

As America has learned, though, the anthrax threat must be fought at many levels. One way is to try to prevent terrorists from getting the spores. Equally important is to enhance protection and survival should *anthracis's* deadly spores be criminally dispersed. That includes techniques to sterilize, e.g., by irradiation, contaminated environments. As biology enters the post-genome era, hope brims from scientists' drawing boards sketched with ideas of futuristic vaccines and antibiotics to diminish anthrax's lethality.

But because it is the toxin that causes death, technological efforts to weaken the toxin would improve chances for survival as antibiotics work to eradicate the invading bacillus from the host. Researchers at Harvard, for example, are developing a synthetic chemical that may decrease the virulence of the toxin. Other researchers are studying the toxin through genetic modification.

The struggle with biological agents is nearly as old as civilization itself. And in the hands of terrorists or rogue states, as President Bush noted, bioweapons pose a threat to civilization.

| *"The technical hurdles and related expenses associated with exposing many people to enough anthrax are daunting."*

The Threat of Anthrax Has Been Exaggerated

Steven Milloy

In the weeks after the September 11, 2001, terrorist attacks, the American people were further alarmed when several people died of anthrax inhalation, and anthrax was discovered in several letters to political and media figures. In the following viewpoint, Steven Milloy argues that contrary to alarmist warnings by some public health officials, terrorists cannot readily use anthrax to easily kill thousands of people. While anthrax spores are easy to obtain, he asserts, it is very difficult to render them into a powder—the deadliest form of anthrax—and even more difficult to deliver such anthrax to mass numbers of people. Milloy, an adjunct scholar at the Cato Institute, is the author of *Junk Science Judo: Self-Defense Against Health Scares & Scams* and the publisher of the JunkScience.com website.

As you read, consider the following questions:
1. How much anthrax does it take to cause a fatal infection, according to Milloy?
2. What technical challenges does the author say would-be terrorists must overcome to utilize anthrax as a biological weapon?
3. What concerns does Milloy express about the public's response to the flu season?

B ioterrorism alarmists view the death earlier this month [October 2001] of a Florida man from anthrax and the more recent detection of a case of anthrax in New York City as validation of their advocacy of panic. Cooler heads view the incident more as a limited biocrime rather than a harbinger of mass bioterrorism.

Such skepticism no doubt arises from the often glossed-over difficulty of using anthrax as a weapon of mass bioterror.

Anthrax is a bacterium that may cause death by inhalation, ingestion or by contact with skin. The most lethal form of exposure is inhalation of anthrax spores, bodies serving as vehicles for the bacterium.

Alarmists say, "One billionth of a gram [of anthrax], smaller than a speck of dust can kill." But one anthrax spore, even thousands of spores will not kill anyone.

Wool sorters inhale 150 to 700 anthrax spores per hour continually without danger. Laboratory studies indicate that about 10,000 spores are necessary to start an infection by inhalation.

Technical Hurdles

As with other toxins, it's the dose that makes the poison. Therein lies the chief difficulty for anthrax as an effective mass terror weapon.

The technical hurdles and related expenses associated with exposing many people to enough anthrax are daunting.

Aum Shinrikyo, the well-financed terrorist group that used nerve gas in the Tokyo subway in 1995, learned this lesson firsthand. The group employed scientists and invested a great deal of money in trying to develop anthrax into a weapon of mass destruction. The effort failed.

Anthrax spores are easy enough to obtain. But before spores can be made into a mass inhalation threat, they need to be converted to a powdered form. Liquefied anthrax would fall to the ground and be ineffective.

Powderizing Anthrax

In contrast to producing spores, powderizing anthrax is no trivial task.

Even assuming would-be terrorists had the technical know-how for producing mass quantities of powdered anthrax—without killing production workers and surrounding populations—the necessary facilities and development would cost hundreds of millions of dollars. Purchasing a few unemployed, ex-Soviet bioweapons experts is not enough.

Not surprisingly, only the U.S. and Russia so far have succeeded in powderizing anthrax for purposes of weaponization.

Iraq[1] is the most expected source of mass anthrax bioterrorism. But Iraq only has anthrax in liquid form.

Anthrax Exposure Advice

Most threats regarding anthrax have proven to be hoaxes. However, in the event of a possible exposure to a powder or other unknown substance with a threat that may indicate anthrax, call 911 and leave the material alone. To prevent infection if you have a skin exposure to the powder or other substance, wash your hands vigorously with soap and water, and shower with soap and water if necessary. Similarly, washing possibly contaminated clothes in the regular laundry will safely remove any possible anthrax. To be inhaled, anthrax spores must first be aerosolized (dispersed in the air) which does not usually occur. In the unlikely event that you do inhale spores, medical evaluation and treatment is needed, usually after spores are identified.

New York State Department of Health, *Communicable Disease Fact Sheet: Anthrax*, 2002.

Even Iraq seems to know its liquefied anthrax is virtually useless. U.N. inspectors found relatively few Iraqi warheads containing anthrax. If Iraq had an effective form of anthrax, it would likely have been found in many more warheads—like the many Iraqi warheads containing nerve gas.

Iraq probably will never have anthrax capability. As Jane's Intelligence Review reported, "The Iraqis would have to maintain rigorous First World standards and not their usual 'make do' efforts."

Powderizing anthrax is not the end of the challenge.

---

1. At the time this article was written, Iraq was under the control of dictator Saddam Hussein. Hussein's regime, long suspected of developing biological weapons, was deposed by U.S.-led military action in 2003.

Once released into the air, spores then become subject to atmospheric conditions. Too much wind will disperse spores into harmless concentrations. Not enough wind and the spores will fall to the ground and not arise again in harmful concentrations.

Airplanes dusting a city would be an unlikely choice for spreading anthrax spores. The few spores entering buildings would mostly settle; the few that didn't would likely be insufficient in concentration to cause infection. Outside, spores would likely fall to the ground or be blown away and rendered essentially harmless.

If enough spores were dropped, some people conceivably may inhale enough to become infected. But in the worst-case, this might happen to dozens, rather than thousands of people. An accidental release of anthrax spores at a Soviet bioweapons laboratory in 1979 resulted in approximately 70 deaths in a metropolitan area of about 1 million people.

Reckless Warnings

In reckless disregard for the prospects of mass anthrax terrorism, American Public Health Association executive director Dr. Mohammad Akhter wrote in *The Washington Post*, "A cloud of anthrax spores drifting over Arlington [Virginia] could kill tens of thousands of Washingtonians within days."

Then there's University of Minnesota epidemiologist Michael Osterholm who told "60 Minutes" that, "What is important is to scare people into positive action."

Here's the real problem that might hit the U.S. in the next couple of months of 2001 because of this "scaring people into positive action."

Flu Scares

Flu season is near. Anthrax infection initially resembles the flu. Physicians and the public are being told not to assume that flu-like symptoms indicate the flu. Anthrax infection should be suspected as well, say the alarmists.

Perhaps more than 100 million people in the U.S. will exhibit flu-like symptoms at some point during this flu season. Should every cough, sore throat, runny or stuffy nose, and headache be treated as a possible case of anthrax infection?

Only if we want to bring our public health system to a grinding halt.

We are—and always will be—vulnerable to limited anthrax attacks, whether by biocrime or bioterrorism. We should minimize and contain these attacks with the sort of rapid response now being exercised in Florida.

But since mass terror with anthrax is improbable, terrorizing the masses is probably unwise.

Periodical Bibliography

The following articles have been selected to supplement the diverse views presented in this chapter.

Sharon Begley et al.	"Unmasking Bioterror," *Newsweek*, October 8, 2001.
Steven M. Block	"The Growing Threat of Biological Warfare," *American Scientist*, January 2001.
Gavin Cameron et al.	"Planting Fear: How Real Is the Threat of Agricultural Terrorism?" *Bulletin of the Atomic Scientists*, September/October 2001.
W. Seth Carus	"Biohazard—Assessing the Bioterrorism Threat," *New Republic*, August 2, 1999.
Anthony Daniels	"Germs Against Man," *National Review*, December 3, 2001.
Carina Dennis	"The Bugs of War," *Nature*, May 17, 2001.
Jeffrey M. Drazen	"Smallpox and Bioterrorism," *New England Journal of Medicine*, April 25, 2002.
Frederick Golden	"What's Next? It Could Be Smallpox, Botulism, or Other Equally Deadly Biological Agents," *Time*, November 5, 2001.
Ruth Levy Guyer and Jonathan D. Moreno	"Bioterror," *Social Education*, March 2002.
Donald A. Henderson	"The Looming Threat of Bioterrorism," *Science*, February 26, 1999.
Bruce Hoffman	"One-Alarm Fire," *Atlantic Monthly*, December 2001.
Milton Leitenberg	"Myths of Bioterrorism," *Family Practice News*, November 1, 2001.
Michael D. Lemonick et al.	"The Next Threat?" *Time*, October 1, 2001.
Ricki Lewis	"Attack of the Anthrax 'Virus,'" *The Scientist*, November 12, 2001.
James P. Lucier	"The Danger of Biological War," *Insight on the News*, October 15, 2001.
Michael G. Massing	"Where Germs Rule," *Nation*, December 17, 2001.
Bruce Shapiro	"Anthrax Anxiety," *Nation*, November 5, 2001.
Lewis M. Simons	"Weapons of Mass Destruction," *National Geographic*, November 2002.

Jonathan B. Tucker   "What the Anthrax Attacks Should Teach Us,"
                            Hoover Digest, Winter 2002.

Jonathan B. Tucker   "An Unlikely Threat," *Bulletin of the Atomic*
and Amy Sands   *Scientists*, July 1999.

USA Today   "Attacks on Food Supply Unlikely to Succeed,"
                            April 2002.

CHAPTER 2

What Nations and Groups Constitute the Greatest Biological Warfare Threat?

Chapter Preface

The list of countries that are suspected of developing biological weapons includes Iraq, Iran, China, Egypt, Libya, North Korea, Syria, and Taiwan. The difficulties of verifying such suspicions can be seen in the case of Iraq. Unlike most nations, Iraq has been subject to international weapons inspections under the auspices of the United Nations. Such inspections were carried out from 1991 to 1998 and were resumed in November 2002. Despite these inspections, the extent of Iraq's biological warfare capabilities is still unknown.

Iraq's unique situation stems from its defeat by a U.S.-led international coalition in the 1991 Gulf War in which Iraq's soldiers were driven from Kuwait, a neighboring country Iraq had attempted to seize. As a condition of surrender, Iraq's leader Saddam Hussein agreed to declare within fifteen days all of his weapons of mass destruction (including biological weapons) and to turn them over to UN officials to be destroyed. Until such destruction was verified, Iraq was barred from selling oil, its most valuable export.

Between 1991 and 1994 inspectors from the United Nations found some circumstantial evidence of an Iraqi biological arms program, but nothing conclusive. During this time Iraq denied having a germ weapons program and called for the inspections to end. In a propitious breakthrough in 1995, however, Hussein Kamal, Saddam Hussein's son-in-law, briefly defected to Jordan and disclosed the existence of a biological weapons program under his purview. Forced to react to these disclosures, Iraqi officials presented to UN inspectors documents they claimed the "traitor General Kamal" had hidden from them. The documents showed that since 1974 Iraq had conducted extensive research into germ weapons; had produced large quantities of weapons including anthrax spores, botulinum toxin, and aflatoxin, a fungal poison; and had placed biological agents into at least 166 aerial bombs and missile warheads. Iraq also said it secretly destroyed all its biological weapons in May or June of 1991—a claim met with doubt by outside experts.

UN inspectors continued to search for biological weapons in Iraq until they were expelled by Hussein's regime in 1998.

In 2002 Iraq readmitted the inspectors after the United Nations passed a new resolution calling for Iraqi disarmament and cooperation. Many experts believe that parts of Iraq's biological weapons program may have gone undetected despite years of inspections. In a January 2003 interim report, chief UN inspector Hans Blix noted that there "are strong indications that Iraq produced more anthrax than it declared, and that at least some of this was retained after the declared destruction date. It might still exist."

A basic problem confronting weapons inspectors is that much biological technology is "dual-use." The equipment and materials needed to make biological weapons are similar or identical to what is used in civilian medical or biotech research facilities. "You can take any vaccine plant or fermentation plant," argues weapons expert Jonathan B. Tucker, "and convert it fairly easily to the production of biological weapons." Such factors can make it easy for a country like Iraq to disguise biological weapons factories.

Although whatever threat Saddam Hussein may have posed to the rest of the world was eliminated when his regime was deposed by U.S.-led military action in 2003, questions persisted even after Hussein's removal regarding the existence and extent of Iraq's biological warfare capacity. The challenges confronted by experts assessing Iraq's programs illustrate the difficulty in ascertaining the state of biological weapons research in the world. If determining what weapons Iraq possesses is problematical, imagine the challenge of appraising the weapons capabilities of other nations without the aid of UN inspectors. However, such information is vital for any general estimation of the threat biological warfare poses to American security and world peace. The authors in this chapter examine some of the leading nations and groups that might be pursuing biological weapons.

> *"Unlike their state sponsored counterparts, non-state actors are much freer from the constraints of retaliation, making them more likely to use biological agents."*

Foreign Terrorist Groups and Rogue Nations Are a Serious Biological Warfare Threat

Frank J. Cilluffo

Frank J. Cilluffo is a special adviser to the president on homeland security. He formerly was a policy analyst with the Center for Strategic and International Studies. In the following viewpoint, excerpted from testimony before the U.S. Senate Committee on Foreign Relations, Cilluffo argues that the United States must prepare for a possible biological warfare (BW) attack. In addition to the dozen or so countries believed to possess or to be pursuing biological weapons, he asserts that terrorist groups and other "non-state actors" may utilize biological warfare against the United States. Religious and ideologically based terrorist groups pose an especially worrisome threat. The United States must work with other nations to prevent countries and terrorist groups from attempting biological warfare, he concludes.

As you read, consider the following questions:
1. Why is a biological warfare attack difficult to detect, according to Cilluffo?
2. Why might non-state actors be more likely to use biological agents than states, in the author's opinion?

Frank J. Cilluffo, testimony before the U.S. Senate Committee on Foreign Relations, September 5, 2001.

Although there is no way to predict with certainty the biological warfare threat to the homeland in the short-term or the long-term, it is widely accepted that unmatched U.S. power (economic, cultural, diplomatic, and military) is likely to cause America's adversaries to favor "asymmetric" attacks over direct conventional military confrontations. These strategies and tactics aim to offset our strengths and exploit our weaknesses. Against this background, military superiority in itself is no longer sufficient to ensure our nation's security.

A major terrorist incident on U.S. soil involving chemical weapons, conventional explosives or most glaringly, biological warfare (BW) agents, would put our emergency management response to the test at the local, state, and federal levels. . . .

Silent Killers

It could take days, or even weeks, for the symptoms of a biological agent to begin to manifest themselves. In the case of a BW attack, the first responder, the very tip of the spear, is likely to be a primary care physician, healthcare provider, veterinarian, agricultural services inspector, or perhaps an entomologist. Given the unheralded nature of these *silent killers*, it would fall upon the public health and medical communities to detect the attack, contain the incident, and treat the victims. The delayed onset of symptoms, coupled with the fact that it is difficult to discern a deliberate BW attack like small pox from a naturally occurring infectious disease outbreak, makes attribution and identification of the perpetrators exceedingly difficult. Moreover, this type of attack can wreak havoc with the public, which must confront fear of the unknown.

Biological weapons can be delivered through several, different means, ranging from using people as carriers of the disease (including person to person infections), covert dissemination such as aerosolization, or via missile. . . .

A successful BW attack on the United States could be a transforming event. Beyond the physical damage and the loss of life, a major BW attack could shake the confidence of our citizens in our government to the core. It potentially threatens our American way of life, tearing at the very fabric of our society. We must grapple with difficult issues such as whether we are protecting America or Americans. Ideally, we are defending both, but no matter how robust our defenses, we will never be able to protect everything, everywhere, all the time, from every potential adversary.

Rogue Nations

In a recent report on biological warfare by the National Intelligence Council, it is stated that over a dozen states are known to possess or are actively pursuing offensive BW capabilities. Perhaps not surprisingly, a majority of the "rogue nations" populate this list. States have a variety of reasons for developing biological weapons: to augment conventional war fighting capabilities, for blackmail, for deterrence/compellence, and/or for prestige.

By way of example, during the [1991] Gulf War, Iraq had warheads containing biological and chemical agents produced and ready for use. Also, according to a forthcoming book by arms control analyst Jonathan Tucker, the Soviet Union deployed warheads with small pox biological weapons on at least four intercontinental ballistic missiles (ICBMs)—the SS-11, SS-13, SS-17, and SS-18. These missiles were intended to kill off any American survivors in the aftermath of a nuclear attack.

One cannot over-generalize about state intentions and possible use and delivery of offensive BW capabilities (research and development vary greatly in terms of pathogen type and associated virulence, toxicity, stability, resistance to detection/treatment, quantity of weaponized agents, and sophistication of means of delivery), which differ from state to state. While the resources available to states to develop biological weapons are much greater than those available to non-state actors, they remain constrained to an extent by the possibility of retribution and retaliation.

For states not inclined to cause mass human casualties and with more discriminate aims, namely to cause economic havoc, we must also consider agricultural bioterrorism (agro-terrorism) against our nation's livestock and/or crops.

Imagine the consequences in your home state if wheat, corn, citrus fruit, potatoes, tobacco, or livestock (to list a few) were the target of a BW attack. As the recent European

71

hoof-and-mouth outbreak demonstrated, pathogens that target agriculture not only cause massive losses to the cattle industry and farmers, but also impact a nation's ability to feed its citizens and disrupt the economy. In addition it upsets free travel and tourism, which are secondary effects, but equally costly. Certainly U.S. borders are porous to bacteria, fungi, viruses, and insects, all of which could be used to attack the nation's food supply.

Terrorist Organizations

While bullets and bombs, not bugs and gas, will remain the weapon of choice for most non-state actors or terrorist organizations, some have expressed interest in seeking to acquire from other states or develop their own offensive BW capability. In my eyes, this represents more of an evolving threat, and although much has been written on the subject, the scientific sophistication needed to sustain and deliver BW agents, if not insurmountable, is substantial, nonetheless the fabrication of a crude BW device and means of delivery, on the other hand is very realistic and difficult to detect or preempt at any time. Moreover, conventional explosives continue to become more lethal and for the most part have been effective in achieving their terrorist aims.

But unlike their state sponsored counterparts, non-state actors are much freer from the constraints of retaliation, making them more likely to use biological agents. After all it is hard to retaliate against an actor if there is no return address. Modern terrorism trends also highlight a propensity toward indiscriminate violence and greater casualties. For example, a hamas [Palestinian terrorist group] training manual expounds that it is foolish to hunt a tiger when there are plenty of sheep to be had. And [terrorist] Usama Bin Laden has publicly pronounced that acquiring weapons of mass destruction, chemical, biological, radiological, and nuclear (CBRN), is a religious duty. Whereas traditionally terrorism was a political tactic, an attempt to get to the negotiating table, some of today's groups motivated by radical religious or nationalist beliefs, no longer seek a seat at the table, but rather want to blow the table up altogether and build their own in its place.

While the likelihood of a catastrophic BW attack on the U.S. homeland, whether committed by state or non-state actors, whether delivered covertly or by missile, remains rela-

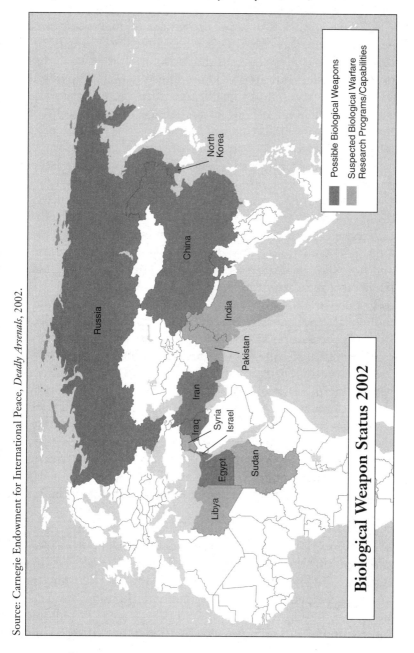

Source: Carnegie Endowment for International Peace, *Deadly Arsenals*, 2002.

tively low in the foreseeable future, the consequences are too high to be ignored. . . .

Time for Cold Evaluation

The United States is now at a crossroads. While credit must be given where it is due, the time has come for cold-eyed assessment and evaluation, and the recognition that we do not presently have—but are in genuine need of—a comprehensive strategy for countering the threat of bioterrorism and the larger challenges of homeland defense. It is important to remember that defense against bioterrorism is but one plate in our counterterrorism armor.

As things presently stand, however, there is neither assurance that we have a clear capital investment strategy nor a clearly defined end-state, let alone a clear sense of the requisite objectives to reach this goal.

Make no mistake, though. The dimensions of the challenge are enormous. The threat of bioterrorism by states and non-state actors presents unprecedented planning challenges to American government and society. . . .

In our view, a complete CBRN [chemical, biological, radiological, and nuclear] counterterrorism strategy involves both (1) preventing an attack from occurring (our first priority should always be to get there before the bomb goes off; or better yet, prevent it from being built in the first place), which includes non-proliferation, counter-proliferation, preemption, and deterrence, and (2) preparing federal, state, local, private sector and non-governmental capabilities to respond to an actual attack. In short, our counterterrorism capabilities and organizations must be strengthened, streamlined, and then synergized so that effective prevention will enhance domestic response preparedness and vice versa. . . .

The Role of Diplomacy

We need to think about ways to reassess arms control measures to limit the proliferation of BW agents, material, and expertise. This cannot be monitored like a START [nuclear arms] agreement or via traditional international conventions, but the United States should take the lead in building international support for multinational activities, while maintaining, and perhaps even codifying, the right to take action, including military action, against violators.

In so doing, though, it must be kept in mind that traditional arms control measures—which assume large state efforts with detectable weapons production programs—are less effective in monitoring smaller proliferation efforts, or even large efforts, as the development of BW capabilities lend themselves to covert production. These will also be more effective vis-à-vis state-sponsors of terrorism than non-state actors. However, by focusing on state actors, we may also capture non-state actors swimming in their wake.

Along with some foreknowledge of the actions of hostile parties, the U.S. should strengthen its partnerships with foreign countries. Bearing in mind the transnational characteristic of the threat, the U.S. would be remiss in trying to address the problem alone.

Diplomacy plays a major role in combating terrorism. Considering the shift away from political terrorism and towards ideologically based terrorism, many countries, the U.S. included, find themselves more at risk. An international interest exists in learning about and dealing with terrorism and there are many states that have already acquired a breadth of knowledge on the subject. The U.S. could draw on many of these countries' experiences, thereby flattening its learning curve.

Moreover, engagement with these nations is critical for antiterrorism and counterterrorism endeavors, where cooperation and understanding provide the keys to success. Most importantly, cooperation works. The Jordanian authorities saved countless American lives during the millennium celebrations by preventing planned attacks on American tourists in the region. Clearly our first line of defense should not be on our shores at the water's edge.

*"A small but growing number of domestic
terrorists could attempt to use biological
weapons."*

Domestic Terrorists Constitute a Potentially Serious Biological Warfare Threat

Jessica Stern

While much attention on biological warfare threats against America has been focused on foreign states such as Iraq and terrorist groups such as al-Qaeda, some people argue that an equal or greater threat may come from domestic extremists and terrorists within the United States. In the following viewpoint, terrorism expert Jessica Stern examines the possibility that domestic terrorists might use germ weapons. Although she believes that the likelihood of such a scenario has been overstated by some, the potential consequences of a bioterrorist attack make it a threat that should not be ignored. She argues that the most likely candidates to use biological weapons are the small but growing number of extreme religious and right-wing groups who are unconstrained by political objectives. Stern, a former National Security Council official, is a lecturer on terrorism at Harvard University's Kennedy School of Government and the author of *The Ultimate Terrorists*.

As you read, consider the following questions:
1. What motivational factors does the author list that might lead terrorists to use biological weapons?
2. What recent developments have made biological weapons easier to acquire, according to Stern?

Jessica Stern, "The Prospects for Domestic Bioterror," *Emerging Infectious Diseases*, vol. 5, July/August 1999, pp. 517–22.

Would domestic terrorists use biological weapons? The conventional wisdom among experts has been that terrorists "want a lot of people watching, not a lot of people dead" and are unlikely to turn to weapons of mass destruction. A new school of thought proposes that improved technology has made biological attacks resulting in hundreds of thousands or millions of deaths all but inevitable. While terrorists are increasingly interested in weapons of mass destruction, proponents of the latter view exaggerate the threat. Using biological weapons to create mass casualties would require more than having biological agents in hand. The terrorists would need to disseminate the agent, which presents technical and organizational obstacles that few domestic groups could surmount. In addition, relatively few terrorists would want to kill millions of people, even if they could.

For most terrorists, the costs of escalation to biological weapons would seem to outweigh the benefits. Most modern terrorists have had substantively rational goals, such as attaining national autonomy or establishing a government purportedly more representative of the people's will. Escalating to such frightening weapons would result in a massive government crackdown and could alienate the group's supporters. Biological weapons are also dangerous to produce. . . . Additionally, some terrorists may perceive moral constraints.

Candidates for successful use of biological weapons represent the intersection of three sets: groups that want to use these weapons despite formidable political risks; groups that can acquire the agent and a dissemination device (however crude); and groups whose organizational structure enables them to deliver or disseminate the agent covertly. The intersection of these sets is small but growing, especially for low-technology attacks such as contaminating food or disseminating biological agents in an enclosed space. Major attacks are also becoming more likely. In the sections that follow, we consider eroding motivational, technical, and organizational constraints.

Motivational Factors

Getting Attention. Some terrorists may turn to biological weapons because they believe it would attract more attention to their cause than conventional attacks. Studies of perceived risk show an inexact correlation between scientists' assessment of risk and the level of fear invoked by risky technologies and activities. Biological weapons are mysterious, unfamiliar, indiscriminate, uncontrollable, inequitable, and invisible, all characteristics associated with heightened fear.

Economic Terrorism. Unlike conventional weapons, radiologic, chemical, and biological agents could be used to destroy crops, poison foods, or contaminate pharmaceutical products. They could also be used to kill livestock. (Conventional weapons could be used for the same purposes, albeit less efficiently.) Terrorists might use these agents to attack corporations perceived to be icons of the target country, for example, by contaminating batches of Coca-Cola, Stolichnaya vodka, or Guinness stout. Terrorists could attempt to disseminate anthrax with the explicit goal of imposing expensive clean-up costs on a target government.

Millenarianism. The millenarian idea is that the present age is corrupt and that a new age will dawn after a cleansing apocalypse. Only a lucky few (usually selected on the basis of adherence to doctrine or ritual) will survive the end of time and experience paradise. Some millenarians believe that the saved will have to endure the 7 years of violence and struggle of the apocalypse, and they want to be prepared. Shoko Asahara, leader of the doomsday cult [Aum Shinrikyo] that released sarin gas in the Tokyo subway in 1995, killing 12, told his followers that in the coming conflict between good and evil they would have to fight with every available weapon. A similar belief system explains the attraction to survivalism by Identity Christians, white supremacists who believe in an imminent Armageddon. . . .

Exacting Revenge or Creating Chaos. Politically motivated terrorists who desire to change societies rather than destroy them might avoid killing very large numbers of people because the political costs would exceed the benefits. Some terrorists, however, want to annihilate their enemies or demolish the societal order. William Pierce, leader of the neo-Nazi organization National Alliance, aims to initiate a worldwide race war and establish an Aryan state. "We are in a war for the survival of our race," he explains, "that ultimately we cannot win . . . except by killing our enemies . . . It's a case of either we destroy them or they will destroy us, with no chance for compromise or armistice." Creating social chaos is thus a worthwhile objective in Pierce's view. . . .

Post-Terrorist Threats

There have been plenty of . . . incidents in which groups of various hues have been found in possession of biological agents.

- In 1972, members of a right-wing group known as "Order of the Rising Sun" were arrested in Chicago with between 30 and 40 kg of typhoid bacteria cultures which they were going to use to poison water supplies in Chicago, St Louis and other cities in the Midwest. Their obsession was the creation of a new master race.

- In September 1984, members of the Rajneesh cult contaminated salad bars in The Dalles, Oregon, with *Salmonella typhi*, which causes typhoid fever. They were trying to influence the outcome of a local election. Nobody was killed but 750 people became ill.

- A US tax protest group called "The Patriots Council" were convicted in February 1995 of possessing 0.7 grams of the toxin ricin—enough to kill 100 people. They had been planning to poison US government agents by smearing ricin on their doorknobs. . . .

Against the background of these and other incidents, it is hardly surprising that a five-month study by the US Senate concluded, in March 1996, that "the threat of a terrorist group using a nuclear, biological or chemical weapon of mass destruction in the United States is real. It is not a matter of 'if' but rather 'when' such an event will occur."

Wendy Barnaby, *The Plague Makers*, 1999.

The Aura of Science. Terrorists may want to impress their target audience with high technology or with weapons that appear more sophisticated than conventional ones. Terrorists may find technology appealing for various reasons. William Pierce, who studied physics at California Institute of Technology, is interested in high-technology weapons. In his novel *The Turner Diaries*, right-wing extremists use nuclear, chemical, biological, and radiologic weapons to take over the world. Pierce believes he can attract more intelligent recruits to his organization over the Internet than through radio or leaflets.

The Copycat Phenomenon. Domestic extremists have shown greater interest in chemical and biological weapons in the last 5 years. For example, in 1998, members of the Republic of Texas were convicted of threatening to assassinate with biological agents President Bill Clinton, Attorney General Janet Reno, and other officials. In May 1995, 6 weeks after the Aum Shinrikyo [sarin gas] incident on the Tokyo subway, Larry Wayne Harris bought three vials of *Yersinia pestis*, the bacterium that causes bubonic plague. No law prohibited Harris or any other U.S. citizen from acquiring the agent. The law has been tightened up since, although many fear it is still not restrictive enough. The Federal Bureau of Investigation (FBI) Director Louis Freeh reports that "a growing number—while still small—of 'lone offender' and extremist splinter elements of right wing groups have been identified as possessing or attempting to develop or use" weapons of mass destruction.

In February 1998, Harris boasted to an informant that he had enough military-grade anthrax to wipe out all of Las Vegas. Eight bags marked "biological" had been found in the back of a car he and his accomplice were driving. Several days later, federal authorities learned that the anthrax Harris had brought to Las Vegas was a vaccine strain not harmful to human health. Nevertheless, the incident frightened many people and sparked a proliferation of anthrax hoaxes and threats in the second half of 1998 continuing into 1999 by groups including Identity Christians and other antigovernment groups, extortionists, anti-abortion activists, and presumed prochoice groups. In many cases, the perpetrator's motives were unknown, but some incidents appear to have been student pranks, demonstrating the extent to which the threat of anthrax has entered U.S. consciousness.

Technical Factors

With the end of the cold war and the breakup of the Soviet Union, weapons of mass destruction and their components have become easier to acquire. Underpaid former Soviet weapons experts may be providing biological weapons and expertise to Iran. South African biological weapons scientists have offered their expertise to Libya. State-sponsored groups are most capable of overcoming technical barriers to mass-casualty attacks, but the sponsor would presumably weigh the risk for retaliation before supporting this type of terrorist attack.

College-trained chemists and biologists could presumably produce biological agents, although they might have trouble disseminating them as aerosols. Microorganisms can be disseminated by air in two forms: as liquid slurries or as dry powders. While producing liquid slurries is relatively easy, disseminating them as respirable infectious aerosols over large open areas is not. Although dry powders can be disseminated far more easily, high-quality powders require substantial development, involving skilled personnel and sophisticated equipment. Milling biological agents would require a level of sophistication unlikely to be found among many domestic terrorist groups. Far more likely are low-technology incidents such as contaminating foods, poisoning livestock, or disseminating industrial poisons in an enclosed space. Such attacks could still be lethal. Major attacks cannot be ruled out; however, governments need to prepare.

Organizational Factors

In the mid-1980s, a little-known survivalist group called The Covenant, the Sword, and the Arm of the Lord (CSA) acquired a large drum of cyanide with the intention of poisoning water supplies in major U.S. cities. At the time, CSA was unusual among terrorist groups in that its sole objective was large-scale murder rather than influencing government policies. CSA overcame two of three large obstacles to successful employment of a chemical agent. It had the motivation to use a chemical agent to kill large numbers and no political or moral constraints. The group had acquired a chemical agent, although not in sufficient quantity to contaminate city water supplies. The group's leaders had not recruited technically trained personnel and chose an unworkable dissemination technique. Moreover, the group lacked discipline and was easily penetrated by FBI. It is unlikely that CSA would make such mistakes if it were operating today, when antigovernment groups are so much more aware of the potential of poison weapons for inflicting mass casualties.

CSA was run as a relatively open compound. Some members wrote articles in local papers espousing antigovernment beliefs, and some worked in neighboring towns. Several former CSA members became informants, often because they hoped to get their sentences reduced for other, unrelated, crimes. In recent years, however, antigovernment groups have become more aware of the danger of penetration by law-enforcement authorities and have devised a new way of organizing themselves called "leaderless resistance." Members are encouraged to act on their own, minimizing their communication with the leadership of the movement. Timothy McVeigh operated according to this model. His bombing of the Oklahoma City Federal Building was originally conceived of by CSA, although it is not clear that McVeigh knew of CSA's earlier plot. If future terrorists with chemical or biological agents act on their own or in small, secretive groups, FBI may have difficulty apprehending them.

One of CSA's objectives was to establish a computerized, nationwide system linking right-wing groups. This goal has been achieved, although CSA is not exclusively—or even principally—responsible for this achievement. The nationwide linking of right-wing groups has implications that have not been adequately appreciated by the law enforcement community. The Internet makes terrorist acts easier to carry out. It facilitates leaderless resistance by allowing leaders of the movement to communicate with sympathizers worldwide without having to meet face-to-face with their followers.

The Likeliest Perpetrators

A small but growing number of domestic terrorists could attempt to use biological weapons in the belief that doing so would advance their goals. The most likely are religious and extreme right-wing groups and groups seeking revenge who view secular rulers and the law they uphold as illegitimate. They are unconstrained by fear of government or public backlash, since their actions are carried out to please God and themselves, not to impress a secular constituency. Frequently, they do not claim credit for their attacks since their ultimate objective is to create so much fear and chaos that the government's legitimacy is destroyed. Their victims are often viewed as subhuman since they are outside the group's religion or race.

Religiously motivated groups are increasing. Of 11 international terrorist groups identified by the Rand Corporation in 1968, none were classified as religiously motivated. By 1994, a third of the 49 international groups recorded in the Rand-St. Andrews Chronology were classified as religious. Religious groups are not only becoming more common; they are also more violent than secular groups. In 1995, religious groups committed only 25% of the international incidents but caused 58% of the deaths.

Identity Christians believe that the Book of Revelation is to be taken literally as a description of future events. Many evangelical Protestants believe in a doctrine of rapture: that the saved will be lifted off the earth to escape the apocalypse that will precede the Second Coming of Christ. Followers of Christian Identity (and some other millenarian sects), however, expect to be present during the apocalypse. Because of this belief, some followers of Christian Identity believe they need to be prepared with every available weapon to ensure their survival.

Organizational pressures could induce some groups to commit extreme acts of violence. Followers tend to be more interested in violence for its own sake than in the group's purported goals, making them less inhibited by moral or political constraints than the leaders. Leaders may have difficulty designing command and control procedures that work. Offshoots of established groups may be particularly dangerous. Groups may also become most violent when the state is closing in on them, potentially posing difficulties for those fighting terrorism. Another factor is the nature of the leader. Charismatic leaders who isolate their followers from the rest of society often instill extreme paranoia among their followers. Such groups can be susceptible to extreme acts of violence.

Asked who he thought the most likely domestic perpetrators of biological terrorism were, John Trochman, a leader of the Montana Militia, said that extremist offshoots of Identity Christian groups are possible candidates, as are disaf- .

fected military officers. Some antigovernment groups are attempting to recruit inside the U.S. military. William Pierce also foresees the use of biological weapons by antigovernment groups. "People disaffected by the government include not only the kind of people capable of making pipe bombs. Bioweapons are more accessible than are nuclear weapons."

A Low-Probability High-Cost Risk

Terrorism with biological weapons is likely to remain rare. This is especially the case for attacks intended to create mass casualties, which require a level of technologic sophistication likely to be possessed by few domestic groups. While state-sponsored groups are most likely to be capable of massive biological weapons attacks, the state sponsor would presumably have to weigh the risk for retaliation. As in the case of other low-probability high-cost risks, however, governments cannot ignore this danger; the potential damage is unacceptably high. Because the magnitude of the threat is so difficult to calculate, however, it makes sense to focus on dual-use remedies: pursuing medical countermeasures that will improve public health in general, regardless of whether major biological attacks ever occur. This would include strengthening the international system of monitoring disease outbreaks in humans, animals, and plants and developing better pharmaceutical drugs.

The risk for overreaction must be considered. If authorities are not prepared in advance, they will be more susceptible to taking actions they will later regret, such as revoking civil liberties. Attacks employing biological agents are also more likely and will be far more destructive if governments are caught unprepared.

"No one knows how committed the Russian military remains to biological weaponry."

Russian Research Programs Are a Potential Wellspring of Biological Weapons Proliferation

Wendy Orent

The Soviet Union maintained a large biological weapons research program throughout the 1970s and 1980s, in violation of the Biological Weapons Convention (BWC) its leaders had signed in 1972. In 1992, one year after the Soviet Union had collapsed and dissolved into Russia and other former Soviet states, Russian president Boris Yeltsin ordered the shutting down of Russia's biowarfare program. However, many observers remain concerned about continuing research in Russia and the possibility that Russian scientists are making biological weapons and selling them to other countries. In the following viewpoint, journalist Wendy Orent describes an ongoing program (begun in 1991) in which American and Russian scientists cooperate in biological research and in dismantling the Soviet bioweapons program. Despite such progress, Orent claims there are indications that Russia is maintaining part of its bioweapons program.

As you read, consider the following questions:
1. What indications exist that Russia is maintaining part of its biological warfare capacity, according to Orent?
2. What examples of past Soviet/Russian deceit does the author describe?

Wendy Orent, "After Anthrax," *The American Prospect*, vol. 11, May 8, 2000.

Poking my head down, looking into the abyss of a four-story-tall, 20,000-liter fermenter, which was one of 10 there to produce anthrax for weapons, made me shudder. It made me wonder, what were they thinking? This was a big facility, [with] just an awesome capability to destroy life. In a mobilization period, it was going to produce and weaponize 300 metric tons of anthrax. *What were they thinking?*"

The speaker is Andrew Weber, the Department of Defense's special adviser for threat reduction policy. He is a clear-eyed, mild-mannered man who has looked into the abyss in more ways than one, but who still has the heart of an idealist. Weber is one of the foremost advocates of Russian and American scientific collaboration. And he was the first to see for himself the gigantic biowarfare plant in Stepnogorsk, Kazakhstan, after the fermenters and the bomblet fill machines were turned off forever. "They ought to turn Stepnogorsk into a bioweapons museum, before they tear it down completely," he says now.

Beating Swords into Ploughshares

At Stepnogorsk, the shining emblem of cooperation between former Soviet biowarfare researchers and American scientists, they are "beating swords into ploughshares," in the words of Alan P. Zelicoff, senior scientist at Sandia National Laboratories in Albuquerque, New Mexico. Zelicoff has received Department of Energy funding for his Aral Sea project, in which American scientists and several former Soviet bioweapons laboratories will jointly monitor the area by using small animals as sentinels, to make certain that the staggeringly huge bioweapons dump at Vozrozhdeniya Island in the Aral Sea is not starting to produce dangerous diseases such as plague, anthrax, or tularemia. "This is a win-win situation," says Zelicoff.

The U.S. Congress is . . . debating . . . various programs whose joint purpose is essentially the same: to divert biological weapons experts from the former Soviet Union into self-supporting commercial and public health enterprises and, perhaps most importantly, to prevent these scientists from "going South"—selling their expertise to Iran, Iraq, Libya, Syria.

How well are these programs working? No one really

knows. "Americans play checkers; Russians play chess," an experienced observer said to me once. "They're always thinking several moves ahead of us."

Despite President Boris Yeltsin's 1992 decree shutting down the Russian biowarfare program, no one knows how committed the Russian military remains to biological weaponry. In its proposed new military doctrine, published in *Krasnaya Zvezda* on October 9, 1999, Russia would reserve the right to use nuclear or "other mass destruction weapons" against its enemies. Furthermore, according to a Stockholm International Peace Research Institute (SIPRI) report on the proposed military doctrine, "Russia would NOT consider itself bound by . . . any disarmament treaty in the case of a critical situation or war." This is worrisome. There are at least three biological laboratories run by the Russian Ministry of Defense that are still closed to the West; while Russian authorities deny that bioweapons research goes on there, we have no way to be certain.

Meanwhile, the U.S. government is contributing money and biogenetic expertise to former Russian bioweapons scientists. Is the technology we are funding furthering research that could be used to make new generations of even more deadly biological weapons? The giant fermenters at various former bioweapons labs may be dismantled—but, in truth, they are no longer needed. Technology developed by American pharmaceutical firms to produce massive quantities of bacteria much more efficiently is now available to Russia. With teams of American scientists now crawling all over Stepnogorsk and Vektor, the lab that once developed an industrial process to produce weaponized smallpox, it is difficult to believe that scientists there are growing weapons strains in secret. But we simply don't know what is going on at the military laboratories.

A Record of Deceit

Certainly the Russian record of deceit is chilling. In 1969 President Richard Nixon shut down the entire U.S. bioweapons program; three years later, the Biological and Toxin Weapons Convention banning research, development, and storage of biowarfare agents was signed by 103 countries, including the United States and the Soviet Union. To the Soviet military, however, the shadow cast by the signing of the bioweapons convention allowed them to proceed swiftly and in secret: They built their program—which had once lagged behind America's—to an unimaginable level. Some 30,000 workers at dozens of laboratories and research institutes worked for Biopreparat, an empire of death that stretched across the Soviet Union.

At the same time, friendly contacts between Western and Russian scientists were beginning to develop. But the Americans didn't quite realize who they were dealing with. The famous Russian virologist Viktor M. Zhdanov, who died in 1987, is still revered as a hero by the people involved with smallpox eradication: He was the first to propose global eradication of the smallpox virus in 1958 at the 11th World Health Assembly in Minneapolis. He also thoroughly charmed his American counterparts. . . .

No one had any idea that this liberal, thinking man was perhaps the principal initiator of bioweapons research in the Soviet Union. In 1973 Zhdanov was appointed by Alexei Kosygin and Leonid Brezhnev as chair of the ultra-secret Interagency Science and Technology Council on Molecular Biology and Genetics. Igor V. Domaradskij, the brilliant, prickly researcher who served as Zhdanov's deputy chair and has since detailed this work in a ruthlessly honest memoir, describes the Interagency Council as the "brains" of the Soviet biowarfare system. By 1975 Zhdanov was forced to resign from the council. Domaradskij insists that the resignation was involuntary and had nothing to do with Zhdanov's lack of enthusiasm for his work. For the rest of his life, Zhdanov worked at Moscow's prestigious Ivanovsky Institute of Virology on research devoted to the study of hepatitis, influenza, and AIDS. According to his wife, virologist Alissa Boukrinskaia, he spoke out passionately against biological weapons.

Boukrinskaia claims not to know that Zhdanov was ever involved in the secret work of the Interagency Council: "Maybe he did not tell me," she said in a telephone interview.

Domaradskij seems amused by that. "We discussed our work at the table, in front of our women. . . . She had to know," he told me.

"Domaradskij is a complicated man; you cannot believe everything he says," insists Boukrinskaia.

Whom to Believe?

When you enter this hall of mirrors, in truth, you cannot make out quite what you are seeing or know how to recognize the guide who can lead you through it. This is a twisted universe, where the man who dreamed of smallpox eradication could design a program that, ultimately, produced weaponized smallpox by the ton. The well-known defector Kenneth Alibek, once second in command of Biopreparat, whose testimony is responsible for most of what we know of the Soviet biowarfare system, once described Russia as "a huge country of liars." The cynic who is philosophically inclined will think at once, rather rudely, of the liar's paradox.

What could Zhdanov have been thinking in 1958, when he proposed eradication? I ask the soft-spoken Alibek. Was his plan to eradicate smallpox deliberate? Did he want to hand the KGB a new weapon, a nonimmune world?

Alibek doesn't think so. "What we need to remember is that Russia is a different country with a different mentality. The same person was quite capable of doing humanitarian and immoral work," he says. "It is strange but true."

Domaradskij agrees. "Each of us," he says, "had to have 'a legend' for the concealment of the true purpose of the work. . . . The legends are used everywhere." . . .

What is truth and what is "legend" today even Domaradskij may not know. Stung by a bitter quarrel with General Nikolai N. Urakov, then as now the head of the bioweapons laboratory at Obolensk, Domaradskij quit Biopreparat in disgust in 1987 and retired. He now describes the entire Soviet biowarfare effort as at once a "big adventure" and a "serious mistake." In 1995 he published his memoir, *Troublemaker*, an account of his life in Biopreparat, at his own expense. It has circulated samizdat-style, and he has suffered for it: For years he was denied a passport by the Russian authorities, ostensibly because he had read a doctoral thesis written by one of his own students that contained classified information.

Domaradskij claims that his old enemy General Urakov is "a fanatic." A former U.S. intelligence officer who knew

Urakov several years ago also trusts him not at all. "The [Clinton] U.S. administration," he told me, "does not want to hear anything bad about the Russians. But they're taking our money and laughing all the way to the secret laboratories."

Worries About Russia

Of all of the nations that have developed biological weaponry, Russia remains the most troubling by far. Despite having signed the 1972 international Biological Weapons Convention along with 139 other nations, the Soviet Union ran the world's most aggressive research and development program for years. The flourishing Soviet program long remained hidden behind a cloak of secrecy and lies. Then Ken Alibek exposed the workings of the Soviet Biopreparat program in his chilling memoir, *Biohazard*. . . .

In his memoir, Alibek recounted heading up the job of "weaponizing" anthrax at Stepnogorsk after earlier successes with tularemia and brucellosis. In fact, Alibek pointed out with pride, he succeeded beyond the dreams of his superiors. Before being officially shut down in 1992, Alibek says, Biopreparat [the Soviet biological weapons program] developed two thousand strains of anthrax alone, as well as bomb- and missile-ready versions of smallpox, the hemorrhagic fever Marburg, plague, and many more. Soviet scientists were even exploring the creation of genetically engineered strains of combination viruses that would defy conventional treatments, and proteins that would cause nerve damage or madness. They produced and replenished ready stockpiles of the most important agents, maintaining a 4,500-metric-ton supply of anthrax at all times.

That last figure stuns William Patrick, who served in the former U.S. biological weapons program in the 1960s. . . .

Russia officially disbanded the biowarfare effort in 1992, but neither Patrick nor Alibek thinks that it was completely destroyed.

Michael T. Osterholm and John Schwartz, *Living Terrors*, 2000.

Public statements by Lieutenant General Valentin I. Yevstigneyev, head of the Fifteenth Directorate, the branch of the Russian military that controls biological "defense," hardly allay these suspicions. In a July 1999 interview in *Yaderny Kontrol*, Yevstigneyev admits that military labs are doing research on the most dangerous pathogens, including the Ebola and Marburg viruses, in order to protect against disease outbreaks. (He does not specify why these tropical diseases would be a threat in Russia.) Marburg was already weaponized at Vektor under the Soviet regime, and no one knows what the military lab at Sergiyev Posad is doing with it now. According to Yevstigneyev, the military work is all defensive. But who, and what, are they defending against?

Domaradskij speculates that the cover stories may have changed, but the secret work has not.

Suspicious Work at Russian Laboratories

How free from military control are the laboratories we support? We know that half the funding at Obolensk State Research Center of Applied Microbiology, where Domaradskij once worked and Urakov is still in charge, comes half from American programs and half from the Russian government. "Obolensk is still pretty close to the mother ship," says an expert on weapons proliferation.

In 1997 the publication of an article in the international journal *Vaccine* by two Obolensk scientists, Andrei Pomerantsev and Nikolai Staritsin, produced a violent reaction both within and outside Russia. The article describes the successful transfer of genes from Bacillus cereus, an organism that does not normally cause human infection, into anthrax. These genes cause hemolysis, or the breaking of red blood cells. Introduced into anthrax, they cause a modified disease for which the present U.S. vaccine probably will not produce immunity. Domaradskij, who was Pomerantsev's mentor, insists that no good interpretation can be put on this experiment.

"He's not their golden boy. I believe they punished him, not for doing the research, but for publishing it," says a knowledgeable American scientist.

The matter of Pomerantsev—whose story, like Zhdanov's, is a multifaceted prism—does not end there. One administration official speculates that Pomerantsev might have wanted to publish to "be helpful, to draw our attention to our vulnerabilities. He has his quirks," the official continues, "but I think favorably of him. This was evil work that was done for the military, but now he's collaborating with us on our anthrax project."

But another American scientist who met Pomerantsev and Staritsin at a conference last August [1999] in Taos, New Mexico, mentions that their latest research abstract takes their earlier genetic engineering research a step further. They can now integrate genetic changes right into anthrax. DNA. Why do they publish this research? The scientist asked Staritsin this straight out and could not get an answer.

Domaradskij, who notes that "Pomerantsev was the best of my associates at Obolensk," states that these are the same techniques he and Pomerantsev once used to engineer antibiotic-resistant tularemia, or "rabbit fever," a frequently fatal infection. "Pomerantsev is between hammer and anvil— the hammer is Urakov and his secret service, and the anvil is the necessity to show that at Obolensk the disarmament is being carried out. One way or another, I believe that Pomerantsev and Staritsin do not have the right to speak the truth."

Still, American scientists plan to work with Pomerantsev and Staritsin on the DNA fingerprinting of anthrax strains. "This work has value for understanding an outbreak and also for studying the evolutionary aspects of anthrax and where it came from," says an American collaborating on the project. "If I thought that this research had a dual use, I wouldn't work with them."

Other Russian scientists connected with Obolensk are more suspect than the ambiguous Pomerantsev. One N. Kislichkin, who has his own firm, called Bioeffect, in Obolensk with offices in Vienna and Moscow, has tried to market genetically modified bacteria, including Domaradskij's own strain of antibiotic-resistant tularemia. His commercial flyer states that his company is ready to "create novel microorganisms of a vaccine group for infections . . . on the basis of your order. We are ready to cooperate in research activities within investigations of virulence factor of different infections."

"I think that anybody could buy Kislichkin's service, even a terrorist," says Domaradskij. . . .

Facilities in Siberia

Far out in western Siberia, the Vektor scientists seem to enjoy greater autonomy from central control. Not that they don't have contact with the military. In the *Yaderny Kontrol* interview, Yevstigneyev states that the head of Vektor Laboratories is collaborating with him on a new vaccine for hepatitis B. But Vektor scientists are highly regarded by their counterparts in the West, and it seems that the walls of suspicion are beginning to crumble. Only two years ago, American scientists who visited Vektor reported treatment they felt was designed to harass them: They were not permitted to walk into many buildings and were threatened with a forced quarantine of several weeks if they did. But streams of recent visitors have received a very different welcome. One administration official who recently wandered into Building 6A, long proscribed to visitors and believed to be a site of active smallpox research, reports broken door seals, crumbling concrete walls, and thick layers of dust everywhere—a building that was decommissioned long ago and left to ruin.

An American scientist who has been to Vektor several times over the past five years reports an intimate conversation he had recently with a well-regarded, but sometimes wary, Russian scientist. The two sat drinking vodka late into the night. At some point, when the Russian was clearly somewhat inebriated, he burst into tears, confessing how happy he was to have the opportunity to work so closely with American scientists. The American sat stunned; later he told me that he believed in his host's sincerity.

Other people laugh. "These are crocodile tears," says Ken Alibek. "Sure he's happy. He's getting paid." Another American official confesses that he is deeply distrustful of late-night drinking sessions with the Russians. "I'm much more likely to believe them when they're stone-cold sober at 10:00 in the morning."

Domaradskij says only that the tears of the nameless Russian scientist were probably heartfelt and sincere: "In Russia it is generally believed that a drunken man tells the truth."

So we have here two groups of scientists, old enemies, who are trying to work together to overcome decades of distrust and the long habit of "legends" and deceit. The progress they are making is not a grand or splendid thing, unless you consider the destruction of giant fermenters to be splendid. It is quiet, slow, and deeply uncertain.

Can you ever trust people who once did such evil work? From our own past come plenty of reasons for uneasiness.

We also had a biological weapons program, which supposedly trafficked in only nonlethal agents, though what is nonlethal to a healthy young soldier supplied with antibiotics might have a very different outcome on the weak, the sick, the old. (According to chemical weapons expert Benjamin C. Garrett of Battelle Memorial Institute, there is no such thing as a truly nonlethal agent—even tear gas can kill.) Our program worked with tularemia among other agents. Biowarfare expert William C. Patrick notes that we developed a strain of tularemia that was resistant to one antibiotic. Domaradskij went the Americans two better; his strain was resistant to three.

The American program was shut down by that peculiar knight in armor Richard Nixon. The bioweaponeers at Fort Detrick faced the ruin of their careers. A former intelligence official tells the story: "Tom Dashiell, Bill Patrick, and a couple of other guys approached a foreign government—not the Soviets. According to Bill, they were really wondering, where do we go from here? This was our life work; this was all we were trained to do."

So our bioweapons experts formed a consortium and approached, in the words of the former officer, "a government which was not unfriendly—then.

"But soon they got a call from the State Department: '*What* are you guys doing?'"

Patrick, the only member of the consortium still active in this field, laughs when he recalls his foray into international trade: "Several of us were in the development area, research, development, and production [of biological weapons]—there was a lot of knowledge among us." Did the State Department put a stop to it? "Oh my lord, yes," says Patrick.

But if we can't rely on the internal moral compass of our own people, how do we trust the other side? Through these dark corridors, it may be that Andrew Weber, with his belief in the ultimate triumph of Russian-American cooperation, has the only flashlight we can follow. It may also be that we are walking blindly, that we are deceived, as trusting American scientists were by Zhdanov. But where else can we go?

"Many international critics convincingly argue the US is a . . . biological weapons control 'rogue state.'"

American Research Programs Are a Potential Wellspring of Biological Weapons Proliferation

Edward Hammond

In 1969 President Richard Nixon pledged that the United States would never use biological weapons. The United States signed the Biological Weapons Convention, prohibiting development and stockpiling of biological weapons, in 1972. But in the following viewpoint, Edward Hammond argues that the United States might be violating the treaty and going back on its pledges. Secret military research programs to develop defenses against biological weapons, destroy drug plants, and develop "nonlethal" weapons of incapacitation involve the creation of what are clearly biological (and chemical) weapons, he asserts. Such programs leave the United States in a weakened position to campaign for biological weapons disarmament. Hammond is director of the U.S. office of the Sunshine Project, an international organization dedicated to biological weapons control.

As you read, consider the following questions:

1. Why do many countries question America's renunciation of biological weapons, according to Hammond?
2. Why is the term "nonlethal weapons" a misnomer, in the author's opinion?

Edward Hammond, "Averting Bioterrorism Begins with U.S. Reforms," *Synthesis/ Regeneration*, vol. 27, Winter 2002. Copyright © 2002 by The Sunshine Project, www.sunshine-project.org. Reproduced by permission.

The United States feels an imminent threat of biological or chemical terrorist attack. How do our own policies relate to the rise of this frightening situation? Why has our government been throwing away so many opportunities to work with other nations to control weapons of mass destruction? In 1983, the US Army estimated that one thousand kilograms (2200 lbs.) of sarin nerve gas aerosolized over an urban area on a clear, calm night would kill 3,000–8,000 people, an attack in terms of human lives roughly proportionate to [the September 11, 2001 terrorist attack] on the World Trade Center. One tenth of the amount of anthrax spores—one hundred kilograms—distributed under similar conditions would be likely to result in the death of 1 to 3 million people, an unimaginable toll 200 to 600 times that in New York.

Once upon a Time

There was a time when the US arguably could muster sufficient credibility to lead a campaign to eliminate chemical and biological weapons. In 1973, President Richard Nixon renounced biological weapons and mostly dismembered the US bioweapons apparatus. It wasn't an altruistic move so much as a way to discourage poorer countries from developing offensive biological warfare capabilities that could rival nuclear weapons in killing power.

Not produced in large quantities for so long that many are actually leaking their deadly contents, old stocks of chemical weapons began to be incinerated at the end of the Cold War (the process continues today). Russian inspectors were even allowed to enter and examine US facilities that they thought might be producing biological weapons. The US ratified the Chemical Weapons Convention, and was in talks with other nations to develop a UN system to verify global compliance with the Biological Weapons Convention.

The Present

There has always been a shadier side to the US renunciation of chemical and biological weapons. For example, Cuban accusations of biological attack with agricultural pests (unproven but stridently alleged and not without evidence), enemies convinced that the US maintains offensive biological weapons (incorrect as alleged, but some biodefense research walks a razor-thin line), and refusal to accept responsibility for the horrendous human and environmental effects of Agent Orange [a chemical defoliant used in the Vietnam War].

The fact that the US maintains what is far and away the largest biological weapons defense program in the world doesn't help either. Even the greatest experts disagree on which specific activities are offensive and which can be classified as defensive. The tendency among governments has been toward classifying all "research" (as opposed to weapons-building and testing) as the latter. The laxity of interpretation has given rise to potential misunderstandings and opened doors to would-be biological weapons developers. Genetic engineering has made matters worse, further blurring the line between offensive and defensive and giving rise to the technical possibility to create genetically-engineered superbugs and even entirely new classes of biological weapons. The billions recently authorized by Congress for homeland defense will swell this opaque military-scientific-corporate biotechnology bureaucracy and the instability it creates to even larger proportions.

Now, many international critics convincingly argue the US is a chemical and biological weapons control "rogue state."

Where did we go wrong? Three main areas: first, fear of terrorism and "rogue states" and, particularly, their access to the military talent and technology of our Cold War enemies; second, missteps retooling the US military for greater involvement in peacekeeping and military "operations other than war" (such as Somalia); third, a foolish attempt to find the ever-elusive "silver bullet" to win the Drug War that has resulted in US development of biological weapons.

Biological Warfare in the Name of America's Children

For more than three years [prior to 2001] the US has menaced other countries with the threat of biological attack. We've mainly harassed two of the world's terrorism hotspots: Afghanistan and Colombia.

The ostensible US motive is to prevent American kids from becoming drug addicts by using biological weapons on

Third World countries that produce the drugs we buy and then snort, inject, and smoke. In Afghanistan the target is opium poppy, [the] source of heroin. Our weapon is a dangerous fungus developed by a perverse alliance of militaristic US drug warriors and ex-Soviet bioweapons researchers who previously dedicated themselves to developing pathogens to destroy US food supplies. The legal pretext includes attempts to gain the "approval" of the Afghan government in exile (in Pakistan), a bitter enemy of the Taliban that has no de facto power. The environmental and human effects of use of these fungi could be devastating.

Our troops are a surprise. This biological weapon is not in our military arsenal but that of the State Department's anti-narcotics division, supported by US diplomatic missions (repeat: diplomatic missions) that provide cash, political, and intelligence support.

The US also supports using bioweapons in other conflict-torn countries, such as Burma and Colombia, site of the largest armed conflict in the Americas. Colombia has no fewer than three terrorist organizations as defined by the State Department, including FARC, one of the world's largest terrorist groups and an organization that has repeatedly killed Americans. It is a testament to the severity of the conflict in Colombia that it has the second largest number of war-displaced persons in the world (after Sudan). Into this mix, the US wants to throw biological weapons.

In case you were wondering, it was proposed here too—to eradicate pot in Florida—but environmental officials immediately shot it down.

"Non-Lethal" Weapons

[The October 3, 1993, incident of] Mogadishu was a harrowing disaster for the US armed forces. Somali civilians literally tore to pieces several US servicemen who thought they were on a mission to help the poor and feed the hungry. The military, understandably anxious to prevent a recurrence, vows it will never happen again. The Pentagon's solution, of course, is not politics but weapons. Specifically, it started a huge program to delve into new and controversial "non-lethal" weapons systems. Non-lethal should not be understood as benign. In fact, these are powerful weapons designed not to prevent death or permanent injury, only to lessen its frequency.

U.S. Research Might Start an Arms Race

The United States appears to have embarked on a largely classified study, across several agencies, of biotech applications for the development of new bioweapons. The clandestine U.S. programs indicate a willingness to ignore treaty law in favor of maintaining technological superiority in response to the emerging bioweapons threat. And U.S. behavior suggests that its biodefense program is even larger than those portions that have been revealed. This U.S. exploration of the utility of biotech for bioweapons development is unwise, for the rest of the world will be obliged to follow suit. In its rush to stay ahead technologically, the United States runs the risk of leading the world down a path toward much-reduced security. More than 30 years ago, the United States ended its offensive bioweapons program in part because it feared that the program's very existence invited other nations to imitate it. That wisdom seems to have been forgotten.

Furthermore, the secrecy required by such a program is antithetical to the transparency on which long-term bioweapons control must be founded. It could also spark a global bioweapons arms race. A world in which many nations are secretly exploring the offensive military applications of biotech would be ripe for proliferation.

Mark Wheelis and Malcolm Dando, *Bulletin of the Atomic Scientists*, January/February 2003.

Apart from microwaves to heat the skin, sound generators to vibrate internal organs, lasers to confuse the eyes, and other non-chemical and biological systems, the Joint Non-Lethal Weapons Program (JNLWP) has entertained proposals to dose people, especially rioters and "potentially hostile civilians," with drugs. These drugs include sedatives, "calmatives" (such as hallucinogens and ketamine, a DEA scheduled narcotic), muscle relaxants, opioids (the class of chemicals in heroin), and "malodorants" (indescribably foul smelling substances). JNLWP has weighed using genetically engineered microbes to destroy enemy vehicles, machinery, and supplies.

It isn't just blackboard and small-scale laboratory work.

The Navy has a genetically modified microbe to destroy plastics and, in the words of one researcher "There is almost nothing some bug won't eat." Delivery mechanisms under consideration or development include backpack sprayers, land mines, mortars, and payloads for unmanned aerial vehicles. JNLWP has planned computer simulations of the offensive use of calmative agents, contracted with a major US military supplier to develop an overhead-exploding chemical riot control mortar round, and field-tested new non-lethal weapons (but not biological ones) on humans in Kosovo.

The Pentagon claims—and desperately wants to hypnotize itself into believing—that these arms are not chemical and biological weapons, rather, that they are a potentially less bloody way to conduct peacekeeping operations, isolate terrorists, and squelch civil disobedience. But it is exceedingly unlikely that people forcibly gassed with mind-altering drugs will view the hijacking of their brains and bodies as a humane act. Much more probably, when their motor control returns and hallucinations fade away, they may have permanent psychological damage and feel enraged at the denial of their freedom of thought and expression.

These are cruel and unusual biological and chemical weapons banned under international laws for arms control, those prohibiting torture, and those for protection of Human Rights. This is how the world, and especially the victims, will understand and react to these weapons if they are used.

Backsliding on the Bioweapons Convention

As 2001 opened, biological weapons control was focused on the completion of six years of negotiations to develop an inspection system to verify global compliance with the Biological and Toxin Weapons Convention, the main international law against biological weapons. The inspection system, called the Verification Protocol, was designed to give teeth to this important international agreement by, among other things, mandating declaration of biodefense research and permitting the UN to inspect suspected bioweapons facilities.

Signs early this year [2001] from the USA were ominous. At a non-lethal weapons meeting in Scotland, US military officers left arms control experts slack-jawed when they called for the renegotiation of the bioweapons treaty to allow the US to produce and use anti-material biological weapons like those being investigated by the Joint Non-Lethal Weapons Program.

In July, bioweapons negotiators were set to meet and try to finalize the verification agreement. The day before the meeting opened, the US press was so uninterested that a back pages *New York Times* headline declared the meeting was taking place in London, more than 450 miles away from the actual site in Geneva, Switzerland.

Unfortunately, the US diplomatic team didn't divert to London and, as expected, arrived in Geneva and trashed the Verification Protocol. The US backed away just as other countries approached agreement. It was reminiscent—and close on the heels—of the US's withdrawal from the Kyoto agreement to control global warming. In this case not content to simply walk away, the US went a big step further. Adoption of the Verification Protocol needs consensus. The US said it will sit in the negotiations and kill the Verification Protocol by deliberately blocking the efforts of others, including the European Union. The United States, standing alone, delivered what may have been a knockout punch to the world's efforts to combat biological weapons cooperatively.

The CIA's Monstrous Mistake

Not everybody at the *New York Times* had been asleep. Although the timing was unusual, in early September [2001], a *Times* article made stunning revelations about the US biodefense program. The US Central Intelligence Agency (CIA) is conducting a secret program of biodefense research that, in the opinion of many experts, violates the Biological and Toxin Weapons Convention. The CIA tested mock biological bombs and built a real bioweapons production facility in Nevada. If any other country conducted this research, it would have drawn the US's harshest denunciations and, quite possibly, military attack. The real reasons for the US rejection of the Verification Protocol suddenly became much more clear.

The CIA's research activities were not disclosed in annual declarations of biodefense activities to the Bioweapons Convention. Without actually mentioning it, the *Times* article incontrovertibly demonstrated that the US had flouted a UN mechanism to enhance transparency and trust between nations. The US remained recalcitrant, claiming the CIA was "entirely appropriate, necessary, consistent with US treaty obligations."

The CIA activities not only threaten arms control; but may have contributed to expanding the black market for bioweapons technology. Part of the CIA effort involved (failed) attempts to buy and then test small biological bombs ("bomblets") manufactured by the Soviet Union in its final years. According to University of Maryland expert Milton Leitenberg:

> CIA operatives would have had to inform various networks of essentially criminal elements—smugglers and middlemen in Russia—of what it was that the Agency was seeking. Those criminal networks would then have tried to obtain the item. If they did not succeed this time, as was apparently the case, they have learned that it is a sought-after commodity, and they may be motivated to continue that effort on their own, understanding that there will be an interested purchaser sometime later. The next time the interested buyer might not be the US CIA.

The Bang of Big Buried Biological Bombs

Next, in mid-September [2001], Dr. Barbara Rosenburg of the Federation of American Scientists dropped another (figurative) bomb detailing the US's disregard for bioweapons control. Rosenburg found Department of Energy documents stating that the US is planning (and might already have begun) to test biological weapons loaded with live agents in two large underground aerosol chambers at the Army's Edgewood Chemical Biological Center in Maryland. A similar facility is suspected to exist for use by researchers pursuing similar aerosol projects at Sandia National Laboratory in New Mexico. Its precise location is unknown. Not by coincidence, Sandia is headquartered at Kirtland Air Force Base near Albuquerque, a major research center for the Joint Non-Lethal Weapons Program.

To the initiated in the technical world of bioweapons research, the kind of research planned is a big no-no. It is of a scale unnecessary for defensive research and apparently designed to yield the exact kinds of data needed to build new biological weapons.

Unfortunately Not the End

Before the Twin Towers crashed to the ground [on September 11, 2001], America's international reputation on control of chemical and, especially, biological weapons was punched full of holes and sinking fast. Staunch allies are appalled. Before September 11, UK officials made less than complimentary remarks to the US press. Australia's Foreign Minister upset [Secretary of State] Colin Powell's otherwise warm and cuddly kangaroo-hop Down Under by blasting US rejection of bioweapons verification at a press conference. If the US's most obedient international lap dogs are biting, it's hard to fathom what could be running through the minds of leaders of many other political persuasions—Iran, Libya, Israel, Sudan, Egypt, Iraq (all accused by the US of developing biological or chemical weapons). Not to mention terrorists. A façade of cooperation between most of these states has been achieved.

But don't be fooled for a minute into thinking that waging war against terrorism will do anything to improve the long-term prospects of avoiding the use of biological and chemical weapons. Key elements of the solution to those problems lie inside our own institutions.

Periodical Bibliography

The following articles have been selected to supplement the diverse views presented in this chapter.

America	"Pro-Life Leaders Condemn Anthrax Threats," November 5, 2001.
Martin Arostegui	"Castro Weaponizes West Nile Virus: Cuban Defectors Say Fidel Castro's 'Biological Front' Studied Ways of Spreading Infectious Diseases Through Birds with Migratory Routes Through the United States," *Insight on the News*, October 1, 2002.
John Barry	"What We Face: The Bottom Line: Saddam Is Years from Getting an A-Bomb, but May Have an Arsenal of Chemical and Biological Weapons," *Newsweek*, September 16, 2002.
Kerry Boyd	"U.S. Attempts to Sink BWC Review Conference," *Arms Control Today*, October 2002.
Francis Boyle	"Bio-Warfare and Terrorism," *Synthesis/Regeneration*, Winter 2003.
Seth Brugger	"U.S. Says Cuba Has Limited Germ Weapons Effort," *Arms Control Today*, June 2002.
Economist	"Know Thine Enemy—Weapons Proliferation; Where the World's Hidden and Not-So-Hidden Nuclear, Chemical, and Biological Weapons Are," February 2, 2002.
Nicholas Kralev	"Cold War in the Hot Zone: U.S. Experts Are Reviewing the Germ-Warfare Capabilities of Other Countries, Including Russia, Which Once Had the Biggest Biological-Weapons Program in the World," *Insight on the News*, December 10, 2001.
Nicholas Lemann	"Whodunit Dept.; the Anthrax Culprit," *New Yorker*, March 18, 2002.
Michael Massing	"Seven Days in October," *Nation*, November 12, 2001.
Jennifer Mendelssohn	"The Winds Of War: Amy Smithson Warns of the Poor Man's A-Bombs, Chemical and Bio Weapons (U.S., Russia, North Korea, Syria, Libya, and Iran Also Have Arsenals)," *People Weekly*, December 14, 1998.
Judith Miller	"U.S. Publicly Accusing 5 Countries of Violating Germ-Weapons Treaty," *New York Times*, November 19, 2001.

Judith Miller et al.	"U.S. Germ Warfare Research Pushes Treaty Limits," *New York Times*, September 4, 2001.
Peter Pringle	"Did the U.S. Start Germ Warfare?" *New Statesman*, October 25, 1999.
Jose Vegar	"Terrorism's New Breed," *Bulletin of the Atomic Scientists*, March/April 1998.
Al J. Venter	"New-Era Threat: Iraq's Biological Weapons," *Middle East Policy*, June 1999.
Aaron Zitner	"Inability to Trace Anthrax Poses Large Security Threat, Experts Say," *Los Angeles Times*, November 21, 2001.

CHAPTER 3

What Measures Should the United States Take to Prepare for Biological Warfare?

Chapter Preface

The crisis began with a patient in an Oklahoma City hospital complaining of fever, aches, and rashes. It turned out to be smallpox—a disease that had not been seen in the United States for more than three decades. By the end of one day, there were thirty-four confirmed or suspected cases of small-pox in Oklahoma, as well as nine in Georgia and seven in Pennsylvania—the apparent work of Iraqi or other terrorists who had released the smallpox virus at shopping malls in those three states. Oklahoma's governor requested that all 3.5 million residents of his state be immediately vaccinated, but because of shortages of the smallpox vaccine, only 100,000 doses were initially provided.

By day six hospitals were overwhelmed with two thousand smallpox cases in fifteen states. Television cameras depicted angry mobs at public health clinics demanding to be vacci-nated; the National Guard was sent to restore order. Some states closed transportation links and tried to prevent out-of-state individuals from entering without proof of recent small-pox vaccination. Food shortages were reported in some cities. Despite the efforts of health officials to isolate smallpox-infected individuals and vaccinate those in contact with them, within two weeks the smallpox epidemic was firmly estab-lished, with at least sixteen thousand infections and one thou-sand deaths in twenty-five states and additional outbreaks in other countries. Some experts predicted 3 million cases (and a million fatalities) within the next ninety days.

Fortunately the events described above did not happen in real life but were part of a wargame simulation conducted in June 2001. The exercise, developed by the Center for Strate-gic and International Studies, the Johns Hopkins Center for Civilian Biodefense Studies, and the Anser Institute for Homeland Security, featured former senior government offi-cials playing various roles (America's president, for example, was played by former Georgia senator Sam Nunn). Partici-pants were presented with "news" about the smallpox out-break and made decisions about how to handle the crisis. Most of them later concluded that the exercise had demon-strated how unprepared the United States was for biological warfare or terrorist acts. Problems ranged from shortages of needed medicines to confusion among local, state, and federal officials over who had authority to deal with the crisis. Dr. Margaret Hamburg, who played the role of the head of the U.S. Department of Health and Human Services in the simulation, said it left the participants "humbled by what we did not know and could not do, and convinced of the urgent need to better prepare our nation against this gruesome threat."

Experts have put forth numerous, varied, and sometimes conflicting ideas on just what the United States should do to prepare for the threat of biological warfare. The articles in this chapter examine various proposals to prevent the tragic outcome of "Operation Dark Winter" from ever becoming reality. As the exercise illustrated, the stakes for preparing for biological warfare are extraordinarily high.

*"Despite a steady media drumbeat . . .
about the specter of terrorist germ attacks
. . . the U.S. remains distressingly ill
prepared to beat back such an assault."*

The United States Must Spend More on High-Tech Defenses Against Biological Warfare

David Stipp

David Stipp is a science writer for *Fortune*, a business news-magazine. In the following viewpoint, written shortly after the September 11, 2001, terrorist attacks that destroyed the World Trade Center in New York and damaged the Pentagon, he writes that the United States is dangerously unprepared for possible acts of terrorism using biological agents such as smallpox and anthrax. America must spend resources on developing cutting-edge diagnostic tools and therapies, increasing its stockpile of vaccines and medicines, and working out plans to coordinate health and safety responses to biological warfare, he argues.

As you read, consider the following questions:

1. What is the problem with lumping biological weapons together with other weapons of mass destruction, according to Stipp?
2. What did a mock bioterrorist attack in Denver reveal about the nation's preparedness, in the author's view?
3. What four measures should be done immediately, according to Stipp?

For Tim and Barb Steier, the owners of a crop-dusting business in Blue Earth, Minnesota, the first aftershock of the World Trade Center and Pentagon attacks [on September 11, 2001] came on the following Saturday. While watching television, they were dismayed to hear a reporter suggest that terrorists might use crop-dusters to release killer substances.

"The next morning," says Barb, "we were shut down"—a federal order temporarily grounded all U.S. crop-dusters. Tim, who is vice president of the National Agricultural Aviation Association, faced more media attention during the following week than a FORTUNE 500 CEO typically gets in a year. Dozens of reporters called to ask about crop-dusting and terror. Steier also spent hours on the phone discussing crop-dusting with the FBI.

The agency's nervous fascination with crop-dusters became understandable once it emerged that terrorists linked to the World Trade Center attacks had sought access to crop-dusters in Florida. It suggested that plans were in the offing—and perhaps still are—for an airborne release of something lethal over an American city. Maybe a deadly chemical like sarin, the nerve gas released in a Tokyo subway in 1995 by the Aum Shinrikyo cult. Or maybe something even worse: a lethal germ like anthrax that could kill not just thousands, as a one-shot chemical attack might, but hundreds of thousands.

Some experts contend that the risk of bioterrorism is very low, citing the rarity of germ assaults and the fact that deadly bugs are tricky to handle and disperse. They may be right, but it is dismayingly easy to make a case for the bioterror possibility. At least one of the World Trade Center hijackers is thought to have had connections with Iraq, a nation known to have produced large quantities of biological weapons, including anthrax. A 1993 federal study reported that spraying about 250 pounds of "aerosolized" anthrax over Washington, D.C., could kill up to three million people—just the kind of vastly more horrible attack the terrorist organization that destroyed the World Trade Center might plan as a follow-up.

The United States Remains Unprepared

Despite a steady media drumbeat in recent years about the specter of terrorist germ attacks—and lots of lip service by policymakers—the U.S. remains distressingly ill prepared to beat back such an assault. The nation doesn't have enough smallpox vaccine to cope with a major release of the fast-spreading disease. Production at the country's only supplier of anthrax vaccines has been stymied for more than a year by quality-control problems. Hospitals, where budgets have been cut to the bone by managed-care practices, have no spare resources to handle the staggering demands of a bio-terrorist attack.

To be sure, anti-bioterrorism spending at the Department of Health and Human Services, the key agency for quelling epidemics, has risen in the past few years—$297 million was appropriated for fiscal year 2001. But so far the federal effort has been "like trying to fill Lake Superior with a garden hose," asserts Michael Osterholm, director of the University of Minnesota's Center for Infectious Disease Research and Policy. That may change because of the [September 11] attack. But it hasn't yet. After Congress appropriated $40 billion in September [2001] for disaster relief and antiterrorist measures, an initial installment of $5 billion was quickly earmarked for various projects. Only one, accounting for a fraction of the $126 million allocated to Health and Human Services, was biodefense-related: Security will be beefed up at federal facilities housing germs that might be used for biowarfare.

"People at the top in Washington are worried about bioweapons, but they tend to lump them with other weapons of mass destruction," says Tara O'Toole, deputy director of the Johns Hopkins Center for Civilian Biodefense Studies. The insidious ability of germs to spread before telltale symptoms appear makes bioterrorism fundamentally different from explosions or chemical attacks. The initial outbreak would be only the start; the spread of infection would unleash ongoing waves of panic.

Many top policymakers wrongly presume that gearing up to deal with explosions and chemical threats will also adequately equip the nation to deal with bioterrorism, asserts O'Toole, who served as Assistant Secretary of Energy for Environment, Safety and Health before joining the university center. Police and firefighters won't be the first line of defense in a biological attack. The horrible burden will fall on hospitals and public health agencies that are hard-pressed even to handle their everyday workloads. "What we need," O'Toole says bluntly, "is a bio-Apollo program."

A Mock Attack

A mock bioterrorist attack in Denver last year [2000] highlighted weak links likely to break after a germ assault. Organized by the Department of Justice, the Topoff exercise called on top officials at government agencies to respond the way they would during a real attack as the drill's planners confronted them with a series of likely unfolding events.

On day one, coping mechanisms were activated much as hoped. As a rash of patients with cough and fever flocked to city hospitals, and hours later began dying, state and federal

---

Necessary Steps

Both health departments and diagnostic labs require greater "surge capacity" to cope with an unexpected disaster. As a first step, disease surveillance capabilities must be bolstered at the state and local levels to provide sufficient staff for round-the-clock emergency operations. The CDC [Centers for Disease Control] should also establish a ready reserve of bioterrorism experts who could be rapidly deployed to an affected city or state in the event of an attack. One approach would be to expand the Epidemic Intelligence Service (EIS), the federal corps of epidemiologists who investigate major disease outbreaks around the United States. . . .

Once an unusual outbreak of disease arising from a covert bioterrorist attack has been detected and diagnosed, the next phase would be to launch an emergency medical response. Given the lack of excess capacity in hospitals today, emergency rooms would be rapidly overwhelmed if large numbers of patients descended on them for treatment. During the 1995 sarin nerve gas attack on the Tokyo subway, for example, more than 85 percent of the people who arrived at hospitals were suffering from anxiety or psychosomatic symptoms, with no evidence of actual toxic exposure. For this reason, a system of mobile medical clinics should be established in each major U.S. city to conduct triage in the aftermath of a bioterrorist attack. The mobile clinics would screen out the "worried well" and refer only seriously ill individuals to hospital emergency rooms for treatment.

Jonathan B. Tucker, *Hoover Digest*, Winter 2002.

---

labs quickly identified an outbreak of plague—the simulated attack had begun when a terrorist covertly released aerosolized plague bacteria at the city's performing arts center. A crack team was summoned from the National Centers for Disease Control and Prevention, state authorities restricted travel around Denver to contain the outbreak, and antibiotics from a national stockpile were rushed to the city.

On day two, things started spinning out of control. Hospitals ran out of beds, antibiotics, and morgue space. Simulated gridlock ensued as panicked masses sought doctors, antibiotics, food, and a way out of town. Precious hours were lost as scores of local, state, and federal officials scrambled to connect and make tough decisions about quarantining patients, allocating scarce antibiotics, and telling the public what to do. At one point a single beleaguered worker found herself assigned to pick up and deal with a mock shipment of antibiotics arriving at the airport from the federal stockpile.

Before she could start counting out pills one by one for thousands of people, she needed to obtain plastic bags for the individualized doses. That led to a six-hour delay as she negotiated the hypothetical gridlock to fetch baggies from Safeway.

By day four, when the drill ended, the simulated situation was dire. Denver had run short on food, rioting had begun, and the disease had spread to other states despite quarantine attempts. Ominously, a sense of hopelessness had set in among many participating officials—even though it was only a drill.

A To-Do List

Topoff and similar drills suggest four things should be at the top of the biodefense to-do list:

• Develop and widely deploy cutting-edge diagnostic tools, such as compact systems that in minutes can identify anthrax, smallpox, and other probable biowarfare agents in blood or sputum samples. For example, Cepheid in Sunnyvale, California, is perfecting a breadbox-sized unit for the U.S. Army that will be able to identify anthrax and other biowarfare agents in less than 30 minutes.

• Rapidly beef up the federal government's pharmaceuticals stockpile so that it has enough vaccines and antibiotics to contain simultaneous outbreaks in multiple cities.

• Organize fire-brigade-like teams of hospital staffers and other workers throughout the country who are trained and equipped to mount fast, coordinated responses to bioterrorism. A recent survey indicated only 20% of U.S. hospitals had plans for dealing with biological and chemical attacks.

• Put in place master plans to coordinate government agencies during bioterror crises, spelling out who will be responsible for what. The plans must address tough social and legal issues, says Kenneth Bloem, a senior fellow at the Johns Hopkins biodefense center. Who will get life-saving doses of scarce antibiotics? What will shield doctors from malpractice suits if they let patients die in a triage situation? Should hospital workers be kept from their families after being exposed to patients with communicable germs?

Fortunately, this biodefense starter kit is on government drawing boards, and elements are already being implemented. But erecting sturdy bioterror shields will require far more funding and political will than have existed to date. The price tag would doubtless be in the billions of dollars—hospital planning alone could well cost over $2 billion, estimates Bloem.

The Smallpox Threat

As bioterror priorities are sorted out, smallpox and anthrax are likely to get the most attention—they appear to pose the greatest risk.

The bad news on smallpox: The virus may have fallen into terrorists' hands as the former Soviet Union's biowarfare program disintegrated. It is hardy, highly infectious, and fatal in about 30% of untreated cases. Routine vaccination for it ended worldwide after 1980—perhaps 20% of Americans have residual immunity from childhood inoculations. In its first few days, a smallpox infection mimics flu; telltale skin lesions typically don't appear for a week or more—plenty of time for an unsuspecting carrier to infect many others.

The somewhat good news: Smallpox vaccinations before exposure confer immunity, and they can attenuate illness in susceptible people if given within four days of infection.

Thus, an outbreak might be contained by rapidly vaccinating people in and around the affected area and quarantining those already infected. Currently [October 2001] the CDC has a stockpile of about 12 million usable doses of vaccine—not nearly enough.

In 2001 the CDC contracted with a British firm, Acambis, to add 40 million doses of a new smallpox vaccine to the U.S. stockpile beginning in 2004. Acambis and the CDC declined to comment on whether the project would be accelerated. "I'd be very surprised if it isn't," says George Washington University microbiologist Peter Hotez, who last year [2000] co-authored an article in the *Washington Post* arguing that at least 100 million doses would be needed to cope with a multi-city outbreak. . . .

Anthrax

Anthrax, unlike smallpox, doesn't spread from one infected person to another. Once inside the body, its rugged bacterial spores can act like time bombs, bursting into fatal action after many weeks of dormancy. Some 90% of those who inhale spores during an attack would probably die if not started immediately on lengthy courses of antibiotics. Early symptoms, typically fever and cough, resemble a cold. After symptoms appear, it's too late—death usually follows within three days regardless of treatment.

As with smallpox, vaccination is the best defense against anthrax. After reports that Iraq and other nations had "weaponized" the bug, the Department of Defense in 1998 launched a program to vaccinate all U.S. military personnel. But vaccine supplies soon dwindled, effectively putting the campaign on hold, after the FDA required that the Defense Department's sole supplier, BioPort in Lansing, Michigan, renovate its plant. The improvements are now in place, and BioPort plans to seek FDA permission this month [October 2001] to start production, said a company spokeswoman. The review process, which ordinarily takes months, could move much faster.

Even after BioPort gets its act together, the threat won't recede quickly. There are currently [as of October 2001] no plans to create a national stockpile of anthrax vaccine for civilian use. Whether a stockpile would help much is unclear anyway—anthrax immunization requires six doses of vaccine given over 18 months, followed by yearly boosters.

New Biodefenses

Better biodefense technologies are on the way. For several years, the U.S. Defense Advanced Research Project Agency has sponsored R&D at commercial and university labs on a wide array of cutting-edge diagnostics and therapies. In DARPA-funded studies at the University of Michigan, for example, an experimental medicine called BCTP was able to protect mice against injections of anthrax-like bacteria. Made of soybean oil and other inexpensive ingredients, the product reportedly can destroy both bacterial and viral biowarfare agents.

It isn't yet clear whether the U.S. will accelerate work on this new wave of biodefenses. But, says a university researcher, "our negotiations [to do research on biowarfare antidotes for the U.S. army] were moving like molasses before Sept. 11. Now they're moving forward at quite a respectable pace." Still, most technology fixes will take at least several years to perfect and widely deploy, says Stephen S. Morse, a Columbia University professor who helped DARPA organize its biodefense initiative.

Meanwhile, let's hope the good guys don't lose track of any crop-dusters.

"Despite all the effort to gear up for biological terror, the problem of overcrowded . . . emergency rooms—where terror's victims would be treated—has received only spotty attention."

Spending More on High-Tech Defenses Will Not Protect Americans Against Biological Warfare

Katherine Eban

Katherine Eban, a former *New York Times* reporter, is an investigative journalist who covers medical and health issues. In the following viewpoint, she argues that the best way for the United States to prepare for a possible bioterrorist attack is to spend more on general improvements to the nation's health-care system. Years of funding cutbacks and managed care have left the nation's hospitals and emergency rooms without the capacity to handle the large-scale emergencies that biological warfare would create. Spending millions of dollars on high-tech defenses against biological weapons while neglecting the basic infrastructure of America's public health system makes little sense, she concludes.

As you read, consider the following questions:
1. What happened to the nation's hospitals between 1980 and 2000, according to Eban?
2. What important and fundamental question has yet to be addressed, in the author's view?

Just before the July 4 holiday this past summer [2002], as National Guardsmen with sniffer dogs monitored the nation's bridges and airports, Jerome Hauer, an assistant secretary at the Health and Human Services Department, dispatched a technician to Atlanta, Georgia, to set up a satellite phone for the new director of the Centers for Disease Control.

If smallpox broke out, if phones failed, if the federal government had to oversee mass vaccination of an urban center, Hauer would have a way to communicate with the CDC director, who since last fall has worked with him on health crises, particularly bioterror. It was one of many precautions that might make the difference between a manageable event and full-scale disaster.

But at the same time, an attempt at crisis management of a more immediate kind was unfolding 2,500 miles to the west. As the FBI chased reports of potential new threats, including a possible attack on Las Vegas, Nevada, Dr. John Fildes, the medical director of Nevada's only top-level trauma center, watched helplessly as a real medical disaster developed, one that had nothing and everything to do with the problems that Hauer was working to solve.

Faced with a dramatic spike in the cost of their malpractice insurance, fifty-seven of the fifty-eight orthopedic surgeons at University Medical Center in Las Vegas resigned, forcing the state's only trauma center that could treat it all—from car crash, burn and gunshot victims to potential bioterror casualties—to close for ten days.

With Las Vegas a potential target, a quarter-million tourists at the gaming tables and the closest high-level trauma center 300 miles away, the crisis barely registered in the federal government. Nevada's Office of Emergency Management (OEP) called to inquire about a backup plan, which, as Dr. Fildes later recounted, was to dissolve the county's trauma system, send patients to less prepared hospitals and take the critically injured to Los Angeles or Salt Lake City, both about eighty minutes by helicopter.

During that anxious week Hauer's satellite phone and Fildes's resignation letters formed two bookends of the nation's disaster planning. Hauer—whose Office of the Assistant Secretary for Public Health Emergency Preparedness

(ASPHEP) was created by the department Secretary, Tommy Thompson, after the anthrax attacks—can get a last-minute satellite phone, a crack staff and even the ear of President George W. Bush on public health concerns.

But Fildes, whose trauma center is the third-busiest in the nation and serves a 10,000-square-mile area, struggles to keep his staff intact and the doors of his center open. And this is in a state with no appointed health director, few mental health facilities, no extra room in its hospitals and the nation's only metropolitan area, Las Vegas, without a public health laboratory within 100 miles. In the event of a public health disaster, like a bioterror attack, Fildes says, "we're prepared to do our best. And I hope our best is good enough."

A Public Health "Train Wreck"

On taking office, President Bush eliminated the health position from the National Security Council, arguing that health, while in the national interest, was not a national security concern. In the wake of the anthrax attacks last year [2001], he changed his tune, declaring, "We have fought the causes and consequences of disease throughout history and must continue to do so with every available means." Next year's budget for biodefense is up 319 percent, to $5.9 billion. States, newly flush with $1.1 billion in biodefense funds, have gone on shopping sprees for emergency equipment like gas masks, hazmat suits and Geiger counters. Newly drafted to fight the war on bioterror, doctors and public health officials are now deemed vital to national security, and their hospitals are even under threat, according to an alert released in mid-November by the FBI.

And yet this flurry of interest and concern has not begun to address America's greatest public health vulnerability: the decrepit and deteriorating state of our healthcare system. In states from Nevada to Georgia, dozens of health officials and doctors told *The Nation* that anemic state funding, overcrowding and staff shortages may be greater problems in responding to bioterror than lack of equipment or specific training. "We don't have enough ER capacity in this country to get through tonight's 911 calls," said Dr. Arthur Kellerman, chairman of the emergency medicine department at the Emory University School of Medicine in Atlanta. Two decades of managed care and government cuts have left a depleted system with too few hospitals, overburdened staff, declining access for patients, rising emergency-room visits and an increasing number of uninsured. The resulting strain is practically Kafkaesque: How do you find enough nurses to staff enough hospital beds to move enough emergency-room patients upstairs so that ambulances with new patients can stop circling the block?

The infusion of cash for bioterror defense without consideration of these fundamental problems is like "building walls in a bog," where they are sure to sink, said Dr. Jeffrey Koplan, the recently departed head of the CDC.

Between 1980 and 2000, the number of hospitals declined by 900 because of declining payments and increased demands for efficiency, according to the American Hospital Association, leaving almost four-fifths of urban hospitals experiencing serious emergency-room overcrowding. Burnout and low pay have left 15 percent of the nation's nursing jobs unfilled, and the staffing shortage has led to a drop in the number of hospital beds by one-fifth; in Boston by one-third, according to the Center for Studying Health System Change in Washington.

Meanwhile, emergency room visits increased by 5 million last year, according to the American College of Emergency Physicians. One in eight urban hospitals diverts or turns away new emergency patients one-fifth of the time because of overcrowding, the American Hospital Association reports. And the costs of health insurance and medical malpractice premiums continue to soar.

Chronic Underfunding

In public health, chronic underfunding has closed training programs and depleted expertise. According to a recent CDC report, 78 percent of the nation's public health officials lack advanced training and more than half have no basic health training at all. During the anthrax crisis inexperienced technicians in the New York City public health laboratory failed to turn on an exhaust fan while testing anthrax samples and accidentally contaminated the laboratory.

A government study of rural preparedness this past April found that only 20 percent of the nation's 3,000 local public health departments have a plan in place to respond to bioterror. Thirteen states have had no epidemiologists on payroll, said Dr. Elin Gursky, senior fellow for biodefense and public health programs at the ANSER Institute for Homeland Security. Meanwhile, 18 percent of jobs in the nation's public health labs are open, and the salaries create little hope of filling them. One state posted the starting salary for the director of its public health laboratory program—a Ph.D. position—at $38,500, said Scott Becker, executive director of the Association of Public Health Laboratories. Becker calls the combination of state cuts and work-force shortages a "train wreck."

Stayskal. © 2002 by Tribune Information Services. Reprinted with permission.

Amid this crisis, clinicians have a new mandate: to be able to fight a war on two fronts simultaneously. They must care for the normal volume of patients and track the usual infectious diseases while being able to treat mass casualties of a terrorist event. They now have some money for the high-concept disaster, but with many states in dire financial straits, there is less money than ever for the slow-motion meltdown of the healthcare system, in which 41 million Americans lack health insurance. In the event of a smallpox attack, the tendency of the uninsured to delay seeking treatment could be catastrophic.

Hauer hopes that the "dual use" of federal resources could herald a golden age in public health, with tools for tracking anthrax or smallpox being used also to combat West Nile virus or outbreaks from contaminated food. But politicians of all stripes continue to propose beefing up biodefense in isolation from more systemic problems. In October, [former vice president] Al Gore argued in a speech that the problem of the uninsured should take "a back seat" temporarily to the more urgent matter of biodefense. And Bush has proposed shifting key public health and biodefense functions into his proposed Department of Homeland Security, a move likely to weaken daily public health work like disease surveillance and prevention, according to the General Accounting Office. A bipartisan report recently issued by the Council on Foreign Relations warned that America remains dangerously unprepared for a terrorist attack, with its emergency responders untrained and its public health systems depleted.

The solution, say doctors, is to tackle the systemic and not just the boutique problems. "If you have a health system that is chaotic and has no leadership and is not worried about tuberculosis and West Nile and just worried about these rare entities, you'll never be prepared," said Dr. Lewis Goldfrank, director of emergency medicine at Bellevue Hospital Center in New York City. "To be useful, money has to be earmarked for public health generally, so that it will prepare you for terrorism or naturally occurring events."

President Bush strongly resisted federalizing airport security until it became clear as day that private security companies and their minimum-wage workers would continue to let a flow of box cutters, knives and handguns through the metal detectors. Some clinicians now say that the specter of bioterror raises a similar question, which almost nobody in Washington has yet begun to address: Has healthcare become so vital to national security that it must be centralized, with the federal government guaranteeing basic healthcare for everyone?

"Forget about paying for the smallpox vaccine," said Dr. Carlos del Rio, chief of medicine at Atlanta's Grady Memorial Hospital. "Who's going to pay for the complications of the vaccine? With what money? We haven't even addressed that. As you look at bioterror issues, it's forcing us to look at our healthcare delivery.". . .

Atlanta's Health Emergency

On September 11, 2001, Dr. Arthur Kellerman was in Washington waiting to testify before Congress about the consequences of uninsurance when a plane struck the Pentagon, across the street from his hotel room. He immediately called back to Grady Memorial Hospital in Atlanta, where he oversees the emergency room residents, and got a disturbing report.

While Atlanta appeared to be safe from terrorism, the emergency room had twenty-five admitted patients waiting for hospital beds, the intensive-care area was packed and the staff had shut the emergency room to new patients. Worse, every emergency room in central Atlanta had declared saturation at the same time. None were taking new patients, and loaded ambulances were circling the block. If attacks had occurred in Atlanta that morning, "there was no way on God's earth we could have absorbed more patients," said Kellerman. Since then, all the Atlanta-area hospitals have gone on simultaneous diversion numerous times, leaving "nowhere to put casualties."

Despite all the effort to gear up for biological terror, the problem of overcrowded and understaffed emergency rooms—where terror's victims would be treated—has received only spotty attention. *U.S. News & World Report* featured the problem as a cover story, "Code Blue: Crisis in the E.R.," but it ran on September 10, 2001. A month after the attacks, Representative Henry Waxman prepared a report on ambulance diversions and their effect on disaster preparedness, finding a problem in thirty-two states. In at least nine states, every hospital in a local area had diverted ambulances simultaneously on a number of occasions, causing harm or even death to some patients. In Atlanta, one diverted patient was admitted only after he slipped into respiratory arrest while in the idling ambulance. The report quoted an editorial from the *St. Louis Post-Dispatch* last year:

> A word to the wise: Try not to get sick between 5 P.M. and midnight, when hospitals are most likely to go on diversion. Try not to get sick or injured at all in St. Louis or Kansas City, where diversions are most frequent. And if you're unlucky enough to end up in the back of an ambulance diverted from one E.R. to another, use the extra time to pray.

In Washington, Hauer has directed each region to identify 500 extra beds that can be "surged" or put into use quickly, which has led a number of states to identify armories, school auditoriums, stadiums and hotels that can be used as MASH hospitals. But no bubble tent can replace a hospital bed, with a full complement of services readily available within the "golden hour" so crucial to treating trauma patients, said Kellerman. And no proposal exists to address the problem as a systemic one, in which a shortage of nurses and cutbacks in reimbursement have made it impossible for hospitals to staff enough beds. . . .

September 11's Hard Lessons

New York City, with sixty-four hospitals, more than any other in the country, was probably the best prepared for a mass-casualty incident. Except that on September 11, most of the victims were dead. Within minutes, the Bellevue emergency room was crowded with hundreds of doctors, each bed with its own team of specialists, from surgeons and psychiatrists to gynecologists. "The entire physician and nursing force of the hospital just came down at once," said Dr. Brian Wexler, a third-year emergency medicine resident. At Long Island College Hospital in Brooklyn, Dr. Lewis Kohl, chairman of emergency medicine, said that by noon, he had a doctor and a nurse for each available bed and could have tripled that number. Doctors from all over the country at a defibrillation conference in downtown Brooklyn were begging to work. "I spent most of the day sending volunteers away," he recalled.

Tragically, so many people died that doctors had little to do. But the people who answered phones, counseled the distraught or drew blood from volunteers were overrun. A web-based patient locator system cobbled together by the Greater New York Hospital Association got 2 million hits within days from frantic relatives. Beth Israel Medical Center ran out of social workers, psychologists and psychiatrists to answer calls. "I answered the phone for half an hour and said, 'I'm not qualified to do this,'" said Lisa Hogarty, vice president of facility management for Continuum Health Partners, which runs Beth Israel.

If anything, New York learned that targeted improvements, such as the creation of regional bioterror treatment centers, will not work. Susan Waltman, senior vice president of the Greater New York Hospital Association, told a CDC advisory committee in June that on September 11, 7,200 people, many covered in debris, wound up at 100 different hospitals, jumping on trains, boats and subways, or walking, to get away from downtown Manhattan. Now imagine if the debris had been tainted with some infectious biological agent. "You can't put the concentration of knowledge or staffing or supplies in regional centers," she said, "because you can't control where patients go."

The anthrax attacks, when they came, were a wake-up call of the worst kind. Baffled government officials with minimal scientific knowledge attributed the outbreak initially to farm visits, then contaminated water and finally to a fine, weaponized anthrax that had been sent through the mail. With no clear chain of communication or command for testing the samples, reporting the results, advising the medical community or informing the public, samples vanished into dozens of laboratories. Conference calls between officials from different local, state and federal agencies were required to track them down, said those involved with the investigation. Testing methods were not standardized, with the Environmental Protection Agency, the postal service, the CDC, the FBI and the Defense Department all swabbing desktops and mailrooms using different methods and different kits, some of which had never been evaluated before. "A lot of those specimens that were said to be positive were not," said Dr. Philip Brachman, an anthrax expert and professor at the Rollins School of Public Health at Emory University.

For three weeks, from the initial outbreak on October 4,

2001, Americans seeking clear information from the CDC were out of luck. Until October 20, the agency's website still featured diabetes awareness month instead of the anthrax attacks. Dr. David Fleming, the CDC's deputy director for science and public health, said that while the CDC did respond quickly and accurately, "we were too focused on getting the public health job done, and we were not proactive in getting our message out.". . .

Preparing for the Worst

Past a strip mall outside Washington, and down a nondescript road, the federal OEP keeps a warehouse of equipment that can all but navigate the end of civilization. It has the world's most sophisticated portable morgue units, each one able to support numerous autopsies. Another pile of boxes unfolds to become a full operating theater that can support open-heart surgery, if need be.

All this equipment can function during "catastrophic infrastructure failure," said Gary Moore, deputy director of the agency. And all of it can be loaded onto a C-5 transport plane and flown anywhere in the world. The federal government has massive resources—twelve fifty-ton pallets of drugs called the National Pharmaceutical Stockpile, which can get anywhere in the country in seven to twelve hours. After the New York City laboratory became contaminated, the Defense Department flew in six tons of laboratory equipment and turned a two-person testing operation into ten laboratories with three evidence rooms, a command center and seventy-five lab technicians operating around the clock.

This monumental surge capacity is crucial to preparedness. So are supplies. Dr. Kohl at Long Island College Hospital, who describes himself as a "paranoid of very long standing," feels ready. He's got a padlocked room full of gas masks, Geiger counters and Tyvek suits of varying thicknesses, most purchased after the anthrax attacks. Pulling one off the shelf, he declared confidently, "You could put this on and hang out in a bucket of Sarin."

But none of this can replace the simple stuff: hospital beds, trained people, fax machines, an infrastructure adequate for everyday use. Indeed, as states slash their public health and medical budgets, the opposite may be happening: We are building high-tech defenses on an ever-weakening infrastructure. In Colorado, for example, Governor Bill Owens cut all state funding for local public health departments in part because the federal government was supplying new funds. Public health officials there suddenly have federal money to hire bioterror experts but not enough state money to keep their offices open. While the Larimer County health department got $100,000 in targeted federal money, it lost $700,000 in state funds and fifteen staff positions. A spokesman for Governor Owens did not return calls seeking comment. States across the country are making similar cuts, said Dr. Gursky of the ANSER Institute, their weakened staffs left to prepare for bioterror while everyday health threats continue unchecked.

From her office window, Dr. Ruth Berkelman, director of Emory's Center for Public Health Preparedness, can see the new, $193 million infectious-disease laboratory rising on the CDC's forty-six-acre campus. While the new laboratory and information systems are needed, she says, if we detect smallpox, it's going to be because some doctor in an emergency room gets worried and "picks up the telephone."

"Public-health laws across the country are highly antiquated."

Reforms of Public Health Laws Are Necessary to Combat Bioterrorism

Lawrence O. Gostin

Lawrence O. Gostin teaches law at Georgetown University and public health at Johns Hopkins University. He directs the Center for Law and the Public's Health, an institute that is part of both universities. In 2001 he supervised the writing of the Model State Emergency Health Powers Act (MSEHPA), a model piece of legislation sponsored by the federal Centers for Disease Control and Prevention (CDC). The legislation was designed to help state governments reform laws governing their response to bioterrorism and other health threats. In the following viewpoint, Gostin defends MSEHPA and argues that public-health laws in most states are antiquated and need to be drastically reformed to enable state and local governments to respond effectively to a biological attack. Gostin argues that the civil and property rights of individuals must be balanced against the common good of public health.

As you read, consider the following questions:
1. How did the September 11, 2001, terrorist attacks change public opinion about safety, in Gostin's opinion?
2. How might existing laws impede an effective public-health response to a bioterrorist attack, according to the author?
3. How does Gostin characterize opponents of his proposed legal reforms?

[T]he September 11, 2001, terrorist attacks on America have] changed the public's perception about the importance of the health, safety and security of the population. Following Sept. 11, the intentional dispersal of anthrax through the U.S. mail increased public concern. America is experiencing a tragedy of unprecedented proportions, but there is one silver lining: The political community is coming together with a clear determination to protect the civilian population from harm.

The draft Model State Emergency Health Powers Act (www.publichealthlaw.net) demonstrates a commitment across party lines to protect the nation against bioterrorist attacks, including an engineered outbreak of smallpox and naturally occurring infectious diseases capable of causing mass casualties. (Smallpox is a disease that is not likely to appear in a naturally occurring form because it was eradicated by an effort from the World Health Organization.) The act was written by the Center for Law and the Public's Health at Georgetown and Johns Hopkins universities at the request of the Centers for Disease Control and Prevention (CDC) to serve as a tool states can use as they review their existing emergency health laws.

Public-health laws across the country are highly antiquated, built up in layers during the last century. Old laws often are outmoded in ways that directly reduce their effectiveness and conformity with modern standards of public-health and constitutional law. For example, most state laws do not require reporting of all the diseases officially recognized as the most likely agents of bioterrorism. The laws may thwart public-health responses by prohibiting communication between federal and state agencies such as public health, law enforcement and emergency management. In other cases, a particular power, such as quarantine, may exist but it does not conform with modern constitutional law. This could result in indecision and litigation in the event of a public-health emergency.

The act addresses these and many other problems in public-health law. In fact, the U.S. Department of Health and Human Services and the Institute of Medicine have called for reform of public-health law. The model law has four major sections, each of which is essential to ensuring preparedness for events such as an intentional dispersal of smallpox. The first two parts—emergency planning and surveillance—are intended to be put into effect as soon as the law passes in each state.

Emergency Planning and Surveillance

The act requires each state to be well-prepared for a public-health emergency. It offers detailed procedures and standards for planning. For example, the states need to think carefully about issues of coordination between federal, state and local agencies, communication to the public and how to handle the logistics of a public-health emergency.

Exercises planned by the federal and state governments before Sept. 11 showed that there was considerable confusion and lack of coordination. One of these exercises, "Dark Winter," involved smallpox; the result was many thousands of projected deaths.

The act requires improved public-health surveillance— the system of careful watchfulness to detect and monitor threats to health. Surveillance is the nation's early-warning system. At present the surveillance system is badly in need of improvement. The model law allows for the kind of monitoring and information-sharing necessary to ensure the public's health. Privacy safeguards are built into the model law. For example, public-health authorities may not disclose the information to employers, insurers, family or friends. But the law would allow sharing, for example, between public-health agencies among the various states (e.g., New York, Connecticut and New Jersey). The law also would permit sharing of data with law-enforcement and emergency-management services, but only where necessary to protect the public's health.

Controls on Property and Persons

The next two powers—managing property and persons— would be exercisable only when the governor declares a public-health emergency. There are many checks and balances on the governor in declaring an emergency. The governor could do so only if there were compelling grounds for believing that there is a strong potential for mass casualties from bioterrorism or a novel infectious disease. It is not intended that long-term endemic diseases such as HIV/AIDS would be covered. The judiciary can review the determination of an emergency. Just as important, the legislature could discontinue the emergency. Thus, the law follows the traditional constitutional role of checks and balances to avoid abuses of power.

The act would permit control of property in a number of

A Confusing Patchwork of Obsolete Laws

Ironically, one reason our public health law is weaker than it was a hundred years ago is that it's largely the same as it was a hundred years ago—but over time societal changes have rendered once-effective laws inadequate. In the late nineteenth and early twentieth centuries, each new disease—cholera, polio, syphilis, tuberculosis—triggered new legislation, granting public health officials specific powers to identify and test the sick, quarantine or treat them as necessary, and require the rest of the population to take preventive measures aimed at stopping the spread of infection. This disease-by-disease approach worked well enough, given the times and the crudeness of medical care, but it has bequeathed us a confusing patchwork of statutes ill-suited to modern threats. Anthrax, for example, can't be passed from person to person. As a result many states' communicable disease laws may not apply to it—which means commissioners might not be able to quickly shut down flights at an airport or stop trains from running if they suspect anthrax has been released. Similarly most state health commissioners can't automatically demand information about lab specimens sent out of state in part because the practice did not exist when the laws were written. Privacy laws enacted in the last two decades prevent public health commissioners from obtaining private medical records on an ongoing basis. They can't actively monitor an uptick in prescription medications, rates of absenteeism from work, or unexplained illnesses and, as a result, they can't always notice an uptick in certain infections. They often lack the power to obtain flight manifests and customer lists, which could be needed in order to track down citizens who have been exposed to an infectious organism. To be sure, state officials can always ask a judge for that authority. But by then it may be too late to prevent a small outbreak from becoming a raging epidemic.

Shannon Brownlee, *The New Republic*, October 29, 2001.

---

ways. These powers are well-established in public-health practice and constitutional law. If a facility such as a subway station or stadium were contaminated and a danger to the public, it could be closed. If an item were contaminated, such as an anthrax-laced piece of clothing, it could be destroyed. These are standard exercises of state governments' "police power" and have been in effect since the founding of the republic.

The law also allows public-health authorities to use goods, services and property for the public good. For example, if a hospital were needed to provide emergency care, the authorities could use it; if a private stockpile of vaccines or pharmaceuticals were needed for the public good, the authorities could use it. These are what are called "takings" in constitutional law. Government may take private property for public goods, provided that they provide compensation. The model law provides property owners the right of due process and it provides compensation for "takings." In this way, the drafters intended the law to be highly respectful of constitutional rights.

Finally, the model law allows public-health authorities to arrange for vaccination, testing, treatment and, if necessary, isolation or quarantine. These infectious-disease-control powers also are well-established in public-health practice and constitutional law. The model law, in fact, provides rights for individuals that do not exist in many current state laws. For example, before issuing a quarantine, public-health authorities usually would have to obtain an order of the court. Once the person was in quarantine, he could have a full due-process hearing. Persons in quarantine would have many new and improved entitlements that simply do not exist in state laws, such as the right to health care, food, clothing and a means of communication with family members and attorneys.

The need for reform has been overwhelmingly supported by the vast majority of people and organizations who have commented. In fact, the model law has been downloaded more than 20,000 times from the Website and has initiated comments from a broad spectrum of citizens, organizations and industries. Certainly there is disagreement on the details; some have urged greater attention to public health, while others have urged greater attention to civil liberties. The drafters respect and encourage this kind of public debate. There always are delicate trade-offs between public health and civil liberties. Only a handful of people have opposed the very idea of public-health-law reform; these comments usually have come from the extremes of the political spectrum. As one governor remarked, "The political left have met the political right in opposition to the model law"—leaving the vast majority of Americans in the middle and unprotected.

Answering Objections

What are the major objections to the law? There are those who oppose the idea of mandatory vaccination, treatment or quarantine. But this is highly problematic from a common-sense perspective. For example, if there were an outbreak of smallpox, clearly there would be a need to vaccinate persons who were exposed or potentially exposed to the virus, as recommended by the Department of Health and Human Services. Similarly, if a person had smallpox, it would be inconceivable that we would allow him to go into a congregate setting such as a school or a workplace. Certainly most people voluntarily would agree to submit to vaccination or quarantine, but some would not. In the event that a person acts in a way that seriously threatens the public's health, it makes sense to ensure the health and well-being of the community.

Others might concede that compulsory powers are sometimes necessary as a last resort, but desire additional safeguards. This is a legitimate, indeed essential, debate. As I have indicated, the draft act sought very hard to respect individual rights provided by due process and patient rights.

Still others are more concerned about property rights. These groups argue that diminution of property rights discourages investment in biotechnology and undermines free enterprise. Private property is worth protecting and society does want to reward innovation. However, in public-health emergencies where the lives of many thousands are at risk, industry should understand the need for a cooperative effort. Owners whose property has been used for public goods are entitled to a hearing under the act and to compensation.

However, the private sector should not be permitted to delay vaccines, drugs and treatment to people in urgent need.

Striking a Balance

Public-health laws and our courts traditionally have balanced the common good with individual civil liberties. As Justice John Marshall Harlan wrote in the seminal U.S. Supreme Court case of *Jacobson v. Massachusetts*, "the whole people covenants with each citizen, and each citizen with the whole people, that all shall be governed by certain laws for the 'common good.'" The model act strikes such a balance. It provides state officials with the ability to prevent, detect, manage and contain emergency health threats without unduly interfering with civil rights and liberties. The act ensures a strong, effective and timely response to public-health emergencies, while fostering respect for individuals from all groups and backgrounds.

> *"Existing laws and individual rights could be suspended."*

Proposed Law Reforms to Combat Bioterrorism Jeopardize Civil Liberties

Twila Brase

In 2001, following the September 11 terrorist attacks, many states debated changes in their public-health laws. In the following viewpoint, Twila Brase argues that many of the reforms debated and in some cases enacted endanger the American public by giving too much power to government and public-health officials, including the power to isolate and quarantine individuals without due process. In addition to the loss of individual liberties, Brase contends that a "command-and-control" approach to public health would alienate the American people and would be ineffective in the event of a biological war or terrorist incident. Brase is president of the Citizens' Council on Health Care, a free-market health-care policy organization based in St. Paul, Minnesota.

As you read, consider the following questions:

1. What are some of the powers granted to public health officials by the Model State Emergency Health Powers Act that Brase has concerns about?
2. According to the author, how might the increased public-health powers under proposed reforms not be limited only to actual bioterrorist incidents?
3. Why might a public-health emergency soon become a crisis of trust between the people and their government, according to Brase?

In the wake of [the terrorist attacks of] September 11 [2001], every state has been asked to enact a law providing for unprecedented, comprehensive health surveillance and medical martial law.

The Model State Emergency Health Powers Act, proposed by the Centers for Disease Control and Prevention (CDC), would provide a state's governor with sole discretion to declare a public-health emergency. Once the emergency was declared, public-health officials would assume police powers, the militia would be mobilized, and the legislature would be prohibited from intervening for 60 days. Any new orders and rules issued by the governor would have the full force of law. Existing laws and individual rights could be suspended.

Broad Authority Proposal

To promote the legislation, state officials and legislators have related it almost exclusively to the threat of bioterrorism. But broader authority is proposed. The new powers would be authorized during any declared public-health emergency. An emergency could be declared with the occurrence or imminent threat of a health condition or illness that is *believed* to be caused by bioterrorism, or the appearance of a novel, previously controlled, or previously eradicated infectious agent or biological toxin. That belief is the only criterion. And although there must be potential for a large number of people to be affected, there is no definition of "large number." The governor, in consultation with health officials, would decide.

The 40-page proposal would require individuals to submit to state-ordered vaccinations, examination, testing, treatment, and specimen collection. Resisters would be charged with a misdemeanor and quarantined. Physicians and other health-care professionals would be required to perform medical procedures or be charged with a misdemeanor.

Quarantine, or isolation, could be imposed without a court order, although an order would have to be obtained "promptly" thereafter. Medical care could be rationed or withheld; private property could be taken or destroyed; compensation for loss of property would be limited; and no person acting under the orders of government officials would be held liable for death, injury, or property damage.

The names, addresses, and physical conditions of, and any other necessary information about, individuals suspected of harboring diseases or health conditions that might have been caused by bioterrorism or an epidemic would have to be reported immediately by doctors and pharmacists. No patient consent or notification would be required.

The public first got wind of the government's plan when the CDC published a draft proposal last October [2001]. What began as a murmur of concern through e-mail soon became a wave of opposition around the country. The Health Privacy Project at Georgetown University took the first shot. It sent a letter to Lawrence Gostin, author of the proposal and director of the CDC's Center for Law and the Public's Health at Georgetown University. The letter attacked the draft's lack of definitions for "epidemic" and "pandemic," terms critical to determining when an emergency could be declared. It also expressed concern over the "breathtakingly expansive scope of the definition of 'public health emergency.'"

Alarming Details

On December 21 [2001], the CDC unveiled its final proposal. Responding to public criticism, the wording had been softened and the definitions made less vague, but there were few substantive changes. In fact, some sections are more egregious than before.

Due process is virtually eliminated. Health officials could pluck citizens out of their homes, place them in quarantine, and need not apply for a court order until ten days later. Nothing specifically would prevent officials from using quarantine or its threat to coerce individuals into submitting to medical procedures they would otherwise refuse. And although a court hearing would be required 48 hours after the court order was received, health officials could request a delay.

Doctors, other health professionals, and health-care institutions would also face coercion. If they refused to follow state-ordered medical directives, officials could strip them of their licenses to practice or operate in the state. On the order of an official, those who take an oath to protect patients might be compelled by state law to harm them (such as by administering a vaccine or performing a high-risk procedure). If a physician questioned directives, followed his conscience, advised citizens to refuse, or obstructed the plans of state officials, he could end up flipping burgers to support his family.

States Have Enough Powers

The short answer to the question of whether states need expanded powers to prepare for a bioterror attack is "no, no way and absolutely not!" The states already have too much power over citizens. . . .

For defense against an unlimited list of unknowable threats, we must choose between the feeble strength of a strong or totalitarian government or the unlimited strength of a free people.

Robert C. Cihak and Michael Arnold Glueck, *Insight on the News*, January 7, 2002.

Additional provisions of the final proposal are just as alarming. Isolation of the sick and quarantine of the exposed must be in different locations, assuring the separation of children and parents. As in the first draft, state officials could ration care, initiate continuing health surveillance, commandeer and control medical supplies, and confiscate personal property. And although the misdemeanor charges were dropped for citizens who don't comply with medical procedures, those who refuse to submit to quarantine and isolation could still be charged with a crime.

The media soon sounded the alarm. By January 2002, the *San Francisco Chronicle* had warned of endangered civil rights. *Investor's Business Daily* called the bill "unhealthy tyranny." *Jewish World Review* said it is a "prescription for disaster," and the *Wall Street Journal* reported that a "new battleground" had been created between health officials and civil libertarians. In early April, *Time* magazine covered the issue of detention powers in an article aptly titled "Mr. Quarantine, meet Miss Liberty."

Public-policy groups began to rally their constituents. The American Legislative Exchange Council (ALEC), a group of

2,400 conservative state legislators, opposed the model act and set up a Web page to track the legislation in every state. The Eagle Forum dedicated an entire radio program to the issue. The Free Congress Foundation denounced the act as a "bad idea." The Association of American Physicians and Surgeons expressed concern about granting governors "dictatorial power." And the Institute for Health Freedom warned of "new state medical police powers."

Proposal Defended

Gostin defended the proposal's purported modernization of the public-health laws. In the December *Insight* magazine he claimed the September 11 attack had one silver lining: "The political community is coming together with a clear determination to protect the civilian population from harm."

In a classic doublespeak, Gostin also claimed that data-privacy safeguards would be in place. But his proposal would permit state public-health agencies to share an individual's medical information with law-enforcement officials, other government agencies, and public-health officials in other states.

The CDC reportedly agreed to pay Gostin $300,000 a year for up to three years to write the model act. He is professor of law at Georgetown and Johns Hopkins universities and sits on the Institute of Medicine's Committee on Assuring the Health of the Public in the 21st Century.

Expanded health powers have long been on Gostin's agenda. The CDC Center for Law and the Public's Health, which he heads, spent the past couple of years culling existing state public-health laws in order to write a uniform comprehensive law that all states could enact. In 1998 Gostin co-wrote a paper proposing that states provide health officials with "a broad and flexible range of powers. By equipping public health authorities with graded powers ranging from isolation, quarantine, and directly observed therapy to cease-and-desist orders or mandated counseling, education, or treatment, authorities will be able to tailor interventions to the specific situation and disease threat."

Health surveillance is the key. To identify emerging health threats, Gostin claims government officials must be empowered to monitor the most minuscule medical details of American life. "If there's a run on anti-diarrhea medications, how would [the federal government] know that?" Gostin asked. Therefore, the health-powers proposal would require an active disease-surveillance system, forcing doctors, hospitals, and pharmacists to share patient data with state health officials.

The Bush administration likes the idea of health surveillance, and in January [2002] the Department of Health and Human Services made $1.1 billion available for bioterrorism preparedness. Federal funding will be directed to, among other things, the development of round-the-clock disease-reporting systems involving hospital emergency departments, state and local health officials, and law enforcement.

[As of August 2002], Arizona, Florida, Georgia, Louisiana, Maine, Maryland, Minnesota, New Hampshire, South Dakota, and Utah have passed versions of the CDC proposal. Nine states—Connecticut, Idaho, Kentucky, Mississippi, Nebraska, Oklahoma, Washington, Wisconsin, and Wyoming—have defeated similar legislation.

Losing Public Trust

The potential effectiveness, or lack thereof, of the CDC's heavy-handed proposal has received little attention. The inauspicious, at times violent, history of martial law has been ignored. Disregarding human nature and all wisdom to the contrary, health officials continue to march a top-down command-and-control proposal across the nation.

Public trust requires thoughtful contingency plans that uphold constitutional rights and freedom of conscience, support medical ethics, and encourage voluntary cooperation with disease containment strategies. State legislatures should not rush to enact ill-conceived, ineffective legislation. Public policy must always recognize and respect the rights, dignity, and intelligence of individuals. An angry public is not a cooperative public. If health officials are empowered to harm the very people legislators want to protect, a public-health emergency may soon become a crisis of the public's trust.

> *"We have no experience at responding to bioterror. But . . . we are good at preventing epidemics through immunization."*

All Americans Should Be Vaccinated Against Smallpox

Louis Warren

Routine smallpox vaccinations of Americans ended in the early 1970s after the deadly disease was successfully eradicated. However, stockpiles of the smallpox virus remain in both the United States and Russia, and some people worry that stolen smallpox germs might be used as biological weapons. In the following viewpoint, Louis Warren contends that the United States is strikingly vulnerable to a smallpox attack and advocates that all Americans once again receive smallpox vaccinations. Warren is a history professor at the University of California at Davis.

As you read, consider the following questions:
1. What lessons does Warren derive from the history of the New World following European contact?
2. How long does a smallpox vaccination retain its effectiveness, according to the author?
3. Why would smallpox be hard to contain after an outbreak, according to Warren?

In the waning years of the Cold War, Russian scientists manufactured tons of the most virulent strain of smallpox in preparation for germ warfare. According to U.S. intelligence officials, some of this material is now in terrorist hands.

U.S. authorities began responding to the threat several years ago, ordering 40 million doses of vaccine to complement the estimated 15 million that remain in warehouses. But new vaccinations won't even be ready until 2004, and there is no plan to administer them unless there is an outbreak.

Lessons of History

How much of a threat is smallpox? The lessons of history are ominous. The civilizations of this hemisphere, formed over thousands of years, were destroyed by disease-causing organisms brought here by Europeans. How did this happen? Indians and Eurasians were separated by oceans for at least 10,000 years. In that time, pathogens evolved in the more populous and more urban Eurasian world that had no counterparts in the Americas. When Old World diseases met New World peoples, epidemics were born. Because American Indians had no immunities to these illnesses, they spread quickly, in what is known as "virgin soil epidemics."

The litany of death from virgin soil epidemics is devastating. The Inca, Maya, Cherokee, Arikara, Mandan, Chumash and hundreds of other peoples saw their populations plummet to one-quarter or less of what they had been. Some peoples disappeared altogether. The political impact was decisive. The Aztec armies numbered 100,000 in 1492. They should have demolished the few hundred Spanish conquistadors who invaded in the early 1500s with their Indian allies, whom the Aztecs had often defeated before. But Spanish illnesses decimated the Aztecs and crushed the spirit of the survivors.

The organisms that did this are well-known killers, including mumps, measles, whooping cough, influenza, diphtheria and bubonic plague. But the greatest of these was smallpox.

Smallpox is extremely contagious. It is carried on droplets in the victim's breath and can kill 30% or more of its victims. In its most virulent form, pustules multiply until the skin rips off the body. Modern science introduced the smallpox vaccination two centuries ago. A worldwide inoculation campaign eliminated the disease in the last third of the 20th century, and in the United States doctors stopped administering the vaccine after 1972.

An Outdated Strategy?

When federal health officials abandoned routine [smallpox] vaccination in 1972, they assumed that "ring vaccination" would be an adequate substitute. The ring strategy involves isolating anyone with a suspected case of the pox, and quickly vaccinating the person's "primary contacts" (friends, family and co-workers) and "secondary contacts" (contacts of the contacts) in an expanding circle. The strategy is an efficient way to contain natural outbreaks. But as Yale health analyst Edward Kaplan observes, "It's a fantasy to believe that the control of small natural outbreaks provides guidance for large bioterrorist attacks." Anyone with the means and motivation to spread smallpox would presumably target a transportation hub or an urban crossroad, not a country store. By the time the first victims developed malaise, fever and rash a week later, others infected at the same time could be dispersed throughout the country.

At the urging of the federal Centers for Disease Control and Prevention, state and local governments are now devising plans to vaccinate *everyone* during a smallpox attack. . . .

Most experts agree that if health departments can pull off what the Feds have in mind, the mass-vaccination strategy will save lives. Smallpox doesn't spread easily from person to person during its seven- to 17-day incubation period, and even infected people can often avoid serious illness if they're vaccinated within four days. Inoculating the nation that quickly would pose enormous challenges, says Kaplan, "but it's not impossible at all."

Geoffrey Cowley, *Newsweek*, October 14, 2001.

Today [in October 2001], a smallpox shot cannot be had for the asking. Each adult who was inoculated as a child has a scar from it, usually on the left shoulder. Although few of us realize it, that's our only token of this medical miracle. The immunity conferred by the vaccine wears off after about 20 years, so virtually the entire U.S. population of more than 280 million would be susceptible. We must ask if the U.S. plan to respond to this threat—a limited supply of vaccine to be dispensed in time of unprecedented emergency—is wise or sufficient.

Smallpox can spread before symptoms, which begin with fever and aches, are recognized. Even when the afflicted began to get sick, few doctors would be able to diagnose this now-unfamiliar killer before thousands, perhaps hundreds of thousands, were infected. Should it be sprayed from an aerosol container aboard a plane or two, it could rapidly spread across the country. Fifty-five million vaccines wouldn't go far.

Good at Immunization

Perhaps American strategists have good reasons for holding back. But a preventive immunization campaign would be a much better idea. We have no experience at responding to bioterror. But as the continuing absence of measles, mumps and diphtheria shows, we are good at preventing epidemics through immunization. Such campaigns are not nearly as difficult as guarding skyscrapers from hijacked jetliners. They are easier and cheaper than patrolling borders, detecting money laundering or finding fugitive terrorists.

The [terrorist] attacks of Sept. 11 [2001] forced us to imagine the unimaginable. And envisioning the horror that might be in our future, we should take heart in remembering that to prevent it, we need only do again what we have done so well in the past. Combating other bioterrors such as anthrax would involve a mere extension of our capabilities for mass immunization.

Terrorists know that a smallpox epidemic won't stop at our borders. Their people are at least as vulnerable as ours. It may be that spreading smallpox hasn't been easy for terrorists to accomplish. We might even have time to inoculate everybody before they can succeed.

*"Vaccination of the entire U.S. population
would result in 600 deaths."*

Not All Americans Need to Be Vaccinated Against Smallpox

Steven Black

Steven Black is codirector of the Kaiser Permanente Vaccine Study Center in Oakland, California. In the following viewpoint, he argues against mass vaccination of all Americans against smallpox. The theoretical risk that a terrorist group or nation might use the smallpox virus as a biological weapon must be weighed against the real health risks that a mass smallpox vaccination would entail, including hundreds of deaths and thousands of serious reactions and injuries. Smallpox vaccinations should only be used in cases where smallpox outbreaks are positively identified, he contends.

As you read, consider the following questions:
1. How deadly was the disease of smallpox, according to Black?
2. Why is the smallpox vaccine more dangerous than other vaccines, according to the author?
3. How does Black describe the "ring" strategy of vaccination?

Immunizations are among the most widely used and effective public health measures. Many immunizations in current use, including those for hepatitis B, polio and whooping cough, have been developed to replace earlier vaccines and provide a more acceptable safety profile.

Because of the continuous safety review process and the application of new technologies in vaccine development, the vaccines we currently use routinely are more effective against more diseases, and are safer than ever.

However, vaccines are not always without dangers.

The vaccine for smallpox was developed at the end of the 18th century and was last routinely used 30 years ago, in the 1970s, before the disease was eradicated worldwide in 1977. The vaccine provides protection against the dreaded risk of smallpox—a disease that killed one out of three people it infected and left most others with lifelong scars or disabilities.

Because of the high risk of smallpox disease and the limits of vaccine technology in the first half of the 20th century, people accepted the dangers associated with routine smallpox vaccination, which were more than outweighed by the ever-present threat of smallpox death.

Small, but Significant Risk of Death

Unfortunately, the smallpox vaccine is just not as safe as any of the other vaccines routinely used in the United States today.

The vaccine injection causes a red, tender and crusting reaction at the vaccination skin site that lasts up to two weeks.

More importantly, one out of 150,000 smallpox vaccination recipients experiences more severe reactions, including overwhelming infection due to the vaccine virus in individuals with abnormal immune systems, encephalitis or brain infection. Another one out of 500,000 individuals will die as a direct cause of the vaccine.

Although the risk of either death or these severe side effects may sound relatively rare, vaccination of the entire U.S. population would result in 600 deaths and 2,000 individuals with serious brain infections. These very real risks must be balanced against what is currently only a theoretical risk of smallpox being introduced by terrorists.

U.S. Smallpox Plan Is Effective

Apart from the hazardous side effects, another reason not to recommend nationwide prophylactic vaccinations is the strong likelihood that the disease can be restrained and managed if an initial case is identified.

The strategy U.S. health officials plan to use is to vaccinate individuals in a "ring" around any cases that are identified, including family, friends, and co-workers. This strategy will effectively control and eventually eliminate infection while exposing the smallest number of people possible to the risks of vaccination.

Flexible Responses

While immunizing or protecting everybody against all possible threats might seem like a logical option, in reality it would not be necessary or desirable. America's high standard of living allows a great deal of flexibility in responding to possible emergencies. . . .

Because of medical advances in supportive medical treatment and the relatively small supply of vaccine now available, we agree with public-health experts who recommend holding off vaccinating the general public against rare or uncommon conditions until there is a demonstrated outbreak. Obviously, stockpiles of emergency vaccine should be widely distributed around the country. . . .

So long as threats remain hypothetical, the general public should not be encouraged or required to risk injury or death from treatments they may never need.

Robert C. Cihak and Michael Arnold Glueck, *Insight on the News*, January 7, 2002.

In addition, it is known that individuals exposed to smallpox can be protected against illness if they are vaccinated within a few days after exposure. Therefore, we have no need to expose the entire U.S. population to the risks of smallpox vaccination with the current vaccine.

It makes much more sense to stockpile enough vaccine to vaccinate only when and if the threat becomes real. This vaccine stockpile can serve as an effective deterrent against terrorism and buy us the time that is needed to develop a safer smallpox vaccine that could be acceptable for general use.

*"Voluntary vaccination could prevent a
smallpox attack from occurring."*

A Voluntary Smallpox
Vaccination Program Is Best

Paul W. Ewald

There has been debate within America's medical community
over whether to reinstitute smallpox vaccinations to protect
Americans against a possible bioterrorist attack. In the viewpoint that follows, Paul W. Ewald proposes that smallpox vaccines be made available to Americans who want to be vaccinated. Individuals can weigh for themselves the potential risks
and benefits of being vaccinated. In addition, he argues, vaccinating even just part of America's population might be enough
to prevent or deter terrorists from attempting smallpox attacks. Ewald is a professor of biology at Amherst College in
Massachusetts and the author of *Evolution of Infectious Diseases*.

As you read, consider the following questions:

1. What government policy regarding smallpox vaccinations
   is Ewald criticizing?
2. How would a partially vaccinated population help
   prevent a smallpox epidemic in the event of a bioterrorist
   attack, according to the author?
3. What factors would people most likely take into
   consideration when deciding whether or not to be
   vaccinated, according to Ewald?

O ur government is now [in 2001] committed to large-scale production of smallpox vaccine as a defense against bioterrorism, but not committed to letting Americans choose to be vaccinated. The plan is to provide vaccines only to those in high-risk groups and to medical workers. For all others, vaccine would be stockpiled until smallpox appeared and then given in a flurry of urgency.

If fears of an attack using smallpox turn out to be much ado about nothing, this approach will have saved Americans from the vaccine's side effects. But what if there is an attack? A fully unvaccinated population could face dangers that would not be easy to control with the crisis approach. But if Americans were given the choice beforehand, when such an attack came many probably would already be vaccinated.

Benefits of a Partially Vaccinated Population

As we saw with anthrax, the first few victims of a bioweapons attack are canaries in the mine. They are more likely to die than those infected later because their infections are advanced when discovered and because those caring for them are just learning how to diagnose, treat and prevent disease in a novel situation. If half the population, for example, chose to be vaccinated now, the number of human canaries would be reduced by half.

A partially vaccinated population would also be a great advantage if attackers released smallpox in more than one place at the same time. A terrorist organization that can release a biological weapon in one location can release it almost as easily in many places. As the number of outbreaks increased, the ability to control the spread by rushing vaccines to the affected areas would certainly decrease, perhaps precipitously.

For individual Americans, there are also issues of varying risk. The risk of being attacked by a bioterrorist may be greater in New York than in Des Moines. It has been greater for postal workers than for the general public and greater for some postal workers than others. Individuals can assess their own unique sets of risks, but if they are denied access to the vaccine, they can't act on those assessments.

When last in use, the smallpox vaccine caused about one death in every million people vaccinated. The risk of serious

Problems with Mass Smallpox Vaccination

As the smallpox vaccine has some nasty side-effects, vaccinating the entire population would not be painless. Approximately 1 out of every 150,000 people would contract severe, debilitating infections and another 1 in 500,000 people would die from the vaccine. So, if all 280 million Americans were vaccinated, more than 500 would almost certainly die. Suddenly, mass vaccination looks less appealing.

Howard Fienberg, "Weighing the Risks of a Vaccine for Smallpox," www.stats.org, July 30, 2002.

nonlethal complications was greater, around one in 10,000.

But these risks can be reduced substantially by assessing risk factors on a person-by-person basis. Pregnancy, for example, poses a risk of side effects for the fetus and increased risks for the mother. A woman who wants to become pregnant might choose to be vaccinated beforehand, so that if an attack did occur, she would not face the grim choice of risking the pregnancy-associated side effects or risking smallpox itself. People with compromised immune systems might also choose to be vaccinated when they could best control the conditions around them.

Ideally, a person who wishes to be vaccinated should also plan the vaccination for a time when he or she will not be in close contact with anyone who is pregnant or whose immune system is suppressed by disease or medications. In a crisis, there would be no time for this consideration.

Perhaps most important, voluntary vaccination could prevent a smallpox attack from occurring. Even if only part of the population were vaccinated, the bang for the terrorist's buck could be drastically curtailed, not only because a smaller number of people would be harmed but also because the spread of the outbreak would be more easily controlled; there would be fewer contagious people and fewer in dire need of immediate vaccination. Terrorists know this. Considering that biological weapons are relatively ineffective, it might not take much vaccination to deter their use.

Americans feel frustrated by terrorism because most can do little if anything to defend against it. Voluntary vaccination would give them some power to protect themselves while helping to deter an attack. Surely many Americans would like to have this choice.

Periodical Bibliography

The following articles have been selected to supplement the diverse views presented in this chapter.

Philip M. Boffey   "Guessing How Quickly a Terrorist Smallpox
                          Virus Could Spread," *New York Times*,
                          December 10, 2002.

Shannon Brownlee   "Under Control—Why America Isn't Ready
                          for Bioterrorism," *New Republic*, October 29,
                          2001.

Eileen Choffnes   "Bioweapons: New Labs, More Terror?"
                          Bulletin of the Atomic Scientists,
                          September/October 2002.

*Christian Science   "Bush's Vaccination Plan," December 13, 2002.
Monitor*

Geoffrey Cowley   "The Plan to Fight Smallpox," *Newsweek*,
                          October 14, 2001.

Mary L. Cummings   "Anthrax and the Military," *Nation*, July 1,
                          2002.

Madeline Drexler   "The Germ Front," *American Prospect*,
                          November 5, 2001.

Julie Louise   "Bioterrorism Preparedness and Response:
Gerberding et al.   Clinicians and Public Health Agencies as
                          Essential Partners," *Journal of the American
                          Medical Association*, February 20, 2002.

Scott Gottlieb   "Smallpox, Big Risk," *American Enterprise*,
                          September 2002.

Bill Hogan   "A Biodefense Boondoggle?" *Mother Jones*,
                          January/February 2002.

*Hospital Case   "Bioterrorism Threat Is New Health Care
Management*   Challenge: Does Our Health System Lack
                          Capacity to Respond?" December 2001.

Alexis Jetter   "What If . . . an Outbreak of Smallpox
                          Threatens to Spiral Out of Control. Can We
                          Contain It?" *Reader's Digest*, February 2002.

Sarah Lueck   "States Seek to Strengthen Emergency
                          Powers," *Wall Street Journal*, January 7, 2002.

Tara O'Toole   "The Problem of Biological Weapons: Next
                          Steps for the Nation," *Public Health Reports*,
                          March/April 2001.

Tara O'Toole, Michael Mair, and Thomas V. Inglesby	"Shining Light on 'Dark Winter,'" *Clinical Infectious Diseases*, April 1, 2002.
Charles V. Pena	"Small Thinking on Smallpox," *Washington Times*, June 20, 2002.
Nancy Shute	"Germs and Guns: Would a Quarantine Work to Control an Epidemic?" *U.S. News & World Report*, November 19, 2001.
Marc Siegel	"The Anthrax Fumble," *Nation*, March 18, 2002.

CHAPTER 4

How Can Biological Warfare Be Prevented?

Chapter Preface

In January 2002 President George W. Bush signed a bill appropriating more than a billion dollars to help states prepare for a biological attack. However, some people argue that biological warfare—much like nuclear warfare—is potentially so devastating that U.S. government efforts should be focused as much on preventing it as preparing for it. Barbara Hatch Rosenberg, a biology professor and peace activist, asserts that preparing for biological warfare "by strengthening public-health response measures is . . . very important, but it is not enough. Prevention must be our goal."

A central component of prevention efforts has been the use of international treaties. In 1925 many nations signed the Geneva Protocol, which banned the military use of biological (and chemical) weapons; the treaty stated that such weapons were "justly condemned by the general opinion of the civilized world." However, that ban only applied to the use of biological weapons, not their possession, and no provisions for inspection or enforcement were included. The United States and other countries continued to research and develop biological weapons in the belief that they needed to be able to retaliate in kind if they were attacked with biological weapons. Some historians have argued that the Geneva Protocol had one unintended effect: it suggested to Japanese military officials that biological weapons must be effective. Consequently, Japan developed a large biological weapons program in the 1930s and waged biological warfare against China during World War II.

At present the linchpin of international efforts to prevent biological warfare is the Convention on the Prohibition of the Development, Production, and Stockpiling of Bacteriological and Toxin Weapons. The treaty, better known as the Biological Weapons Convention (BWC), was submitted before the United Nations in 1972 and has been signed by more than 140 nations, including the United States. However, like the Geneva Protocol, the BWC has been hampered by a lack of stringent enforcement mechanisms. It has proven extremely difficult to check whether countries that have signed the agreement are in fact keeping their pledge not to develop or stockpile biological weapons. "Other [international] agreements on nuclear and chemical weapons have established technical systems for monitoring compliance," notes science journalist Richard Stone. "But the BWC remains little more than an agreement based on trust." Revelations that Iraq and the former Soviet Union have in the past pursued large-scale biological weapons programs after signing and ratifying the BWC have raised further doubts about the treaty's effectiveness. The articles in this chapter offer various perspectives on how to strengthen the BWC as well as other ideas on how to prevent nations from resorting to biological warfare.

"The Biological Weapons Convention is an integral component of arms control."

The United States Should Accept the Biological Weapons Convention Protocol

Council for a Livable World

The Council for a Livable World (CLW) is a lobbying and education organization that advocates arms control and nuclear disarmament. In the following viewpoint, excerpted from a "Fact Sheet" on biological weapons, the council argues that compliance with the 1972 Biological Weapons Convention (BWC), which formally outlawed biological weapons, has been hampered by lack of enforcement mechanisms and by problems in monitoring biological weapons development. The viewpoint's authors criticize the administration of President George W. Bush for derailing long-standing efforts to strengthen the oversight and enforcement mechanisms of the BWC by adding a legally binding protocol to the treaty. They insist that the BWC, with its proposed additions, is an integral means of preventing future instances of biological warfare.

As you read, consider the following questions:
1. What examples of twentieth-century biological warfare does CLW describe?
2. Why has the Biological Weapons Convention (BWC) fallen short of a comprehensive solution to the problem of weapons proliferation, according to the authors?
3. What reasons does CLW give for supporting the BWC Protocol?

The threat of biological war has existed for centuries. By definition, biological warfare involves any deliberate use of disease to attack humans, plants, or animals. Biological weapons have only occasionally been used, but they have the potential to inflict great harm. Unlike the materials necessary to produce nuclear weapons, microorganisms, toxins, and viruses that are dangerous to human, animal, and plant life can be found abundantly in nature. The technology needed to turn these agents into weapons is less sophisticated than what is necessary to develop nuclear weapons. Furthermore, only a very small quantity of material is needed, much less than that needed to produce nuclear weapons, but could potentially cause a comparable death-toll. . . .

History of Biological Weapons Control

The use of biological agents in war has been rare, but dates back hundreds of years. One of the first known instances occurred in 1346 and 1347 when Mongols catapulted corpses contaminated with plague over the wall into Kaffa, a city in Crimea, which forced the besieged Genoans to flee the city. Other states took notice of these methods, and between 1456 and 1767 there were cases of biological warfare involving Belgrade, Russia, and Britain. Aware of the devastating effects of biological weapons, on April 24, 1863, the United States War Department issued General Order 100, which proclaimed the use of poison to be excluded from all modern warfare. However, it was not until July 29, 1899 that the Hague Convention with Respect to Laws and Customs of War on Land was signed, prohibiting the use of poisoned arms. This marked the first true step towards biological arms control.

Despite the passage of the Hague Convention, from 1916 to 1918, Germany used anthrax and equine disease to infect livestock being exported to Allied forces. This prompted a discussion on further measures to be taken to prohibit the use of biological weapons. Following the conclusion of World War I, on June 17, 1925, the Geneva Protocol for the Prohibition of the Use in War of Asphyxiating, Poisonous or Other Gases, and of Bacteriological Methods of Warfare was signed. Japan, however, failed to sign it and the United States did not ratify the protocol.

Between 1937 and 1940, Japan began work on an offensive biological weapons program. In three years, the Japanese killed 10,000 prisoners through biological experiments. During this period, Japan also poisoned the Soviet water supply with an intestinal typhoid bacteria and dropped rice and wheat mixed with plague-carrying fleas over China.

In 1942, shortly after entering World War II, the United States began its offensive biological weapons program. During the war, Germany poisoned reservoirs in Bohemia with raw sewage. Closure of the war did not bring an end to the United States' interest in biological weapons. The United States continued to further develop its program. From September 1950 to February 1951, the United States tested dispersal methods by spraying San Francisco with non-lethal biological simulants.

Testing continued in 1966, when the United States again released harmless biological simulants, this time into the New York City subway system, exposing the city's vulnerability to biological attack. On November 25, 1969, after concluding that biological weapons were neither as accountable or effective as conventional arms, President Richard Nixon announced his plans for the unilateral disarmament of the United States' offensive biological weapons programs. In 1970 he extended this disarmament to include toxins and launched negotiations on an international treaty to ban these weapons.

On April 10, 1972, a critical day for biological arms control, the Convention on the Prohibition of the Development, Production and Stockpiling of Bacteriological (Biological) and Toxin Weapons and on their Destruction (BWC) was opened for signature. Three years later, the United States ratified the 1925 Geneva Protocol along with the BWC. . . .

Summary of the Biological Weapons Convention

The Biological Weapons Convention, an expansion of the 1925 Geneva Protocol, was the first treaty to formally outlaw an entire category of weapons of mass destruction. The treaty was opened for signature on April 10, 1972 and entered into force upon ratification on March 26, 1975. The Biological Weapons Convention is unlimited in duration. To date, there are 164 signatories and 146 ratifications and accessions. The Convention bans the "development, production, stockpiling, and acquisition of biological agents and toxins of types and quantities that have no justification for prophylactic, protective or other peaceful purposes" in addition to "all weapons, equipment, and delivery vehicles designed to use such agents or toxins for hostile purposes or in armed conflict." The Biological Weapons Convention also prohibits the transfer of or assistance in obtaining any of the previous listed agents, toxins, weapons, and equipment.

Though the Biological Weapons Convention was the first treaty to formally ban an entire category of weapons, it is far from a comprehensive solution to the threats presented by biological weapons. One major drawback is that the Convention does not include any measures for enforcing compliance. Over history, the Convention has proven itself unable to prevent violations by its member states. Members that have breached the Convention include Russia and Iraq, and it is suspected that Cuba, North Korea, Iran, Libya and Syria may have as well. Over the 27 years since its entry into force, the number of countries that possess or are actively pursuing biological weapons has increased from 5 to an estimated 11, which includes several member-states to the Convention.

One of the major challenges faced by the Biological Weapons Convention is that biological weapons, by their design, are much more difficult to monitor than nuclear or chemical weapons. Absolute verification of the peaceful use of biological agents is virtually impossible because many of the materials have a dual-use that makes them effective for both biological weapons programs or for legitimate commercial uses.

The following is a list of explanations for why the BWC is more difficult to monitor and enforce than both nuclear and chemical weapons treaties.

1. Chemical weapons need to be produced in multi-ton quantities for use as weapons, whereas biological weapons require only a minuscule amount of material to be militarily significant.

2. Chemical warfare agents, such as mustard gas and sarin, have no commercial use and can therefore be banned. Bio-

logical pathogens and toxins, however, have a variety of peaceful and defensive functions such as protective vaccines and tools in biomedical research for the military. Toxins such as botulinum, used in Botox, has therapeutic applications in medical practice as well.

3. The Biological Weapons Convention forbids the possession of biological agents for military purposes but it does allow for their peaceful scientific, therapeutic, and defensive purposes. Compliance therefore depends on subjective assessment of intent.

4. Most advanced biopharmaceutical plants use a "clean-in-place" system, which rinses pipes with chemicals and hot water, thus eliminating all traces of biological agents within just a few short hours. Short-notice inspections, therefore, may have difficulty discovering evidence of unauthorized production.

5. Improvements in fermentation technology make discovery of covert production of biological agents at dual-capable facilities increasingly difficult. Modern fermentation facilities are capable of producing significant quantities of pathogens in only a few days.

Steps to Strengthen the BWC

Despite the many challenges faced by the Biological Weapons Convention, it remains an integral component to protect against biological warfare. Since the days of President Nixon, there has been bipartisan support for adding measures to the BWC to strengthen prohibition of biological weapons and nonproliferation. In 1986, parties to the Biological Weapons Convention established an annual exchange of information regarding bio-defense programs and maximum-containment laboratories. Under the direction of former President George Bush, the United States made an effort to broaden the exchange of information and also participated in a verification feasibility study conducted by VEREX (the Ad Hoc Group of Technical Experts to Identify and Examine Potential Verification from Scientific Standpoint). This study continued into the Clinton Administration, and VEREX concluded that measures are available to strengthen the Biological Weapons Convention.

Between March 1992 and September 1993, members of the Convention met on multiple occasions to discuss potential methods of verification for the treaty. An Ad-Hoc group was created in 1995 with the goal of developing new measures that would include a legally binding protocol to strengthen the Convention and promote greater compliance. Member-states believed that the development of a system of formal declarations and inspections would increase the transparency of activities and facilities relevant to the treaty, resulting in greater support for and confidence in the BWC.

The Clinton Administration

President Clinton's administration recognized that the Biological Weapons Convention Protocol could not offer a complete solution to the biological weapons problem, but also acknowledged that it would establish legally binding procedures for pursuing evidence that states or individuals were working on the production of offensive biological arms. Clinton spoke out in favor of the Protocol, as it would provide new information that would work to enhance the ability of the United States to detect illegal foreign programs. His administration worked to ensure that the protocol would achieve these objectives without jeopardizing military commercial interests.

The Clinton Administration wanted to achieve the earliest possible conclusion of a BWC protocol that would strengthen international security, but did not give the issue high enough priority to guarantee its conclusion. Instead, the issue was delegated to mid-level agency officials who were left with the responsibility of shaping the U.S. position on important aspects of the protocol. This resulted in political deadlock, and the creation of a BWC Protocol fell under the charge of President George W. Bush.

The BWC Protocol

In April 2001, a draft of the Biological Weapons Convention Protocol was completed. The draft of the Protocol focused on two issues. First, it addressed the need to bolster confidence in compliance with the Convention. Second, the draft dealt with the need to strengthen provisions regarding biological-related cooperation for peaceful objectives. The Protocol attempts to improve cooperation by providing states that do not perceive a biological weapons threat with many incentives to join the Convention. The compliance elements of the Protocol involve the creation of a monitoring regime. There are four major components outlined by the regime:

1. Mandatory declarations of facilities and activities that could most easily be misused to develop biological weapons.

2. Consultation procedures to clarify questions that might arise from these declarations, including the possibility of on-site inspections.

3. Randomly selected transparency visits to promote accurate declarations.

4. Challenge investigations to pursue concerns that a country is developing, producing, or using biological weapons.

The Bush Administration

Shortly after entering office, President George W. Bush requested a policy review of the text provided by the Chairman of the Protocol committee. The review cited 38 problems with the text and recommended that the United States oppose the Protocol. . . .

President George W. Bush announced in July 2001 his administration's plans to oppose the text as well as any subsequent Protocol efforts because it was arguably "too weak and too strong," not capable of catching cheaters while putting U.S. bio-defense research and trade secrets at risk.

The review conference met in November 2001 with little success in completing the long sought-after protocol to strengthen the transparency and verification procedures of the Biological Weapons Convention. At this meeting, the United States emphasized a need to develop more effective measures to deal with treaty noncompliance. On November 1, 2001, President Bush made a statement on the U.S. proposal for the future of the Biological Weapons Convention. He expressed his commitment to strengthening the BWC as part of an all-encompassing plan to fight the threats posed by weapons of mass destruction and terrorism. The President proposed several alternate courses of action for all parties to the Convention.

Previously suggested proposals were based on voluntary efforts, which the United States found unacceptable. On the last day of the conference, the United States tried to disband the Ad Hoc committee. Member parties feared the complete failure of many years of work on the Protocol and in a final effort to save it, they agreed to disband until November 2002.

Rejected Treaty Contains Safeguards

An effective monitoring regime would not require divulging our specific defensive strengths and weaknesses; the draft [BWC Protocol] treaty rejected by the White House contains multiple safeguards for confidential national security and commercial information.

By rejecting the treaty, the Bush administration has implicitly acknowledged its value for exposing questionable activities and thus for deterring violations of the ban. Most of the countries of the world believe that the treaty is badly needed to fill a major gap in global security arrangements.

In their hostility to international treaties, administration officials like to say that only the bad guys should be subject to rules. Evidently, the administration prefers no rules to any that would bind the U.S. But the "good guys" will suffer along with the rest of the world if disease, which recognizes no boundaries, is loosed as a weapon.

Barbara H. Rosenberg and Milton Leitenberg, *Los Angeles Times*, September 6, 2001.

Despite his rejection of the Biological Weapons Convention Protocol, the anthrax attacks in the fall of 2001 prompted the Bush Administration to request increases in funds to protect against bio-terrorism. The Administration asked for an additional $11 billion for bio-defense and preparedness programs over the next two years. This request included $5.9 billion (increased from $1.4 billion) to finance improvements in the nation's public health systems, $1.8 billion for federal agencies involved in bio-defense, $1.6 billion for state agencies and local health care systems, and $650 million to expand the national stockpile of vaccines. (*New York Times*, February 2002) Large spending increases were also requested in the areas of emergency response personnel, border security, and information technology and security.

The increased funding for these programs may help to limit the damage of an attack. However, unlike the Biological Weapons Protocol, such measures do nothing to prevent an attack from happening in the first place.

Arguments for Strengthening the BWC

The Biological Weapons Convention is an integral component of arms control. While the Convention is weak in its verification measures, there is no reason to believe that it cannot be strengthened in the future. The Protocol, which President Bush hastily rejected, was the product of years of research by experts and members of the Ad Hoc committee and has many merits that are worth noting.

First, it is important to recognize that the Protocol was never intended to provide total verification of the BWC. The Protocol's intended purpose was to increase the degree of transparency, thereby helping to deter states from pursuing a biological weapons program in the first place.

Second, the Protocol serves as part of a larger, and more comprehensive plan to battle the proliferation of biological weapons. The Protocol complements intelligence sources, diplomacy, and military power and is designed to draw one's attention to suspicious actions and to encourage follow-up measures in response to these concerns.

The Protocol also enhances the fight against bio-terrorism as it works to prevent proliferation of biological weapons. By eliminating the source rather than focusing on plans to deal with the aftermath of a terrorist attack, the Protocol is a proactive step in defending our nation.

Fourth, the randomly selected transparency visits that would be required by the Protocol would serve as a deterrent against the acquisition of biological weapons. Under the Protocol, proliferators at declared plants would be subject to potential challenge investigations which would deter them from pursuing illicit activities.

The BWC Protocol strengthens the Convention's requirement to encourage scientific and technological cooperation to work for the prevention of disease and for peaceful purposes. It also enhances verification procedures by divulging the capabilities of declared facilities, and then allows for a team of experienced inspectors to determine the nature of activities based on the known capabilities.

Finally, among its Western allies and every country in Latin America, the United States stood alone in its rejection of the Chairman's text. By opposing the Protocol, the United States took a stance more extreme than those taken by Cuba, China, Libya, Pakistan, and Iran, all of which voiced their objections to the text but never formally rejected it. The anthrax attacks in 2001 should make the United States wary of its vulnerabilities. Rejecting the Biological Weapons Convention Protocol only prolongs the period in which states and actors can pursue biological weapons with little to no consequences. A Princeton Research Services poll conducted on Nov. 26, 2001 showed that 79% of Americans supported mandatory inspections of bio-weapon-capable facilities and 71% supported the creation of an international agency with enforcement powers. . . .

The potential threat of a biological attack against the United States is one that should not be ignored. . . . While the Biological Weapons Convention must be strengthened, particularly in the areas of verification procedures and compliance, it remains an effective and necessary step towards reducing these risks.

"Traditional arms control measures . . . applied to biological activities yield no benefit and actually do great harm."

The United States Should Reject the Biological Weapons Convention Protocol

John R. Bolton

In 2001 international negotiations to add a legally binding protocol—which would improve enforcement mechanisms—to the 1972 Biological Weapons Convention (BWC) broke down, in large part because of U.S. objections. In the following viewpoint, excerpted from a 2002 speech in Japan, U.S. undersecretary of state for arms control and international security John R. Bolton argues that traditional arms control approaches are ineffective against biological weapons and that proposed additions to the BWC would have compromised America's national security and business interests. He contends that the United States remains committed in its efforts to prevent the spread of biological weapons despite its rejection of the treaty.

As you read, consider the following questions:

1. How many countries are pursuing biological weapons, according to Bolton?
2. What makes biological weapons more difficult to detect than nuclear and chemical weapons, in the author's view?
3. As listed by Bolton, what steps has the United States taken against the threat of biological weapons proliferation?

John R. Bolton, address to the Tokyo American Center, Tokyo, Japan, August 27, 2002.

I am honored to be here at the Tokyo American Center in Japan and pleased to be able to speak to you about the U.S. position regarding the Biological Weapons Convention, the international treaty that prohibits the development, production, stockpiling and acquisition of biological weapons. Over three decades ago, the United States foreswore biological weapons and became a driving force in negotiating the BWC. The United States strongly supports the global norm established by the BWC and places high priority on combating the threat posed by biological weapons. We continue to be a strong supporter of this treaty.

The threat from biological weapons is real, growing, and extremely dangerous, and is evolving rapidly with the pace of technology. Given the deadly potential of such weapons of mass destruction, as President George W. Bush has said, "there is no margin for error, and no chance to learn from our mistakes."

A Growing Threat

The United States believes that over a dozen countries are pursuing biological weapons. These BW programs are at various stages of development. Some pose a considerable international security threat. Unrepentant rogues, such as [Iraq's leader] Saddam Hussein, continue to seek illegal weapons to sow massive destruction on civilian targets with complete disregard to the BWC and other international agreements. Iran, Libya, Syria, and North Korea are also pursuing these illegitimate and inhumane weapons. There are still other states with covert BW programs that we have not named in Biological Weapons Convention fora. The United States has spoken to several of these states privately. . . . We have also noted that Cuba has at least a limited, offensive biological warfare research-and-development effort. Terrorist groups are actively seeking the knowledge, equipment, and material necessary for biological weapons.

In 1995, Japan experienced the most deadly terrorist attack in its modern history from the Aum Shinrikyo cult, which released sarin nerve gas into a rush-hour subway train in Tokyo, killing 12 and sickening thousands of others. In addition to its chemical warfare capabilities, the cult was later implicated in several smaller-scale attacks with biological agents, including anthrax and botulism, which it launched prior to the attack on the subway.

And last year [2001], soon after the September 11 terrorist attacks, the United States was further terrorized by anthrax attacks that were sent using plain envelopes and 34-cent stamps. Twenty-three people contracted anthrax, and 5 people lost their lives.

Both events showed the world how much serious damage could be done in both physical and psychological terms by even a single person or small group with limited means but with access to biological or chemical weapons. All that was required to inflict harm and widespread panic in both cases was the relevant knowledge, the right materials, and the opportunity.

In the aftermath of these events and of the attacks of September 11, the United States is more determined than ever to put an end to terrorism and to stop the spread of weapons of mass destruction. We are grateful for Japan's unwavering support and cooperation in this effort. As partners in the war against terrorism, we must work together to ensure that those who seek to use disease as a weapon are never allowed access to the materials or technology that will assist them in their aims.

Problems with the Draft Protocol

Some have questioned the U.S. commitment to combat the biological weapons threat due to our rejection of the draft BWC Protocol. Put simply, the draft Protocol would have been singularly ineffective. The United States rejected the draft protocol for three reasons: first, it was based on a traditional arms control approach that will not work on biological weapons; second, it would have compromised national security and confidential business information; and third, it would have been used by proliferators to undermine other effective international export control regimes.

Traditional arms control measures that have worked so well for many other types of weapons, including nuclear weapons, are not workable for biological weapons. Unlike chemical or nuclear weapons, the components of biological warfare are found in nature, in the soil, in the air and even inside human beings. The presence of these organisms does not necessarily connote a sinister motive. They are used for many peaceful purposes such as routine studies against disease, the creation of vaccines, and the study of defensive measures against a biological attack. Components of biological weapons are, by nature, dual use. Operators of clandestine offensive BW programs can claim any materials are for peaceful purposes or easily clean up the evidence by using no more sophisticated means than household bleach. Detecting violations is nearly impossible; proving a violation is impossible. Traditional arms control measures are based on detecting violations and then taking action—military or diplomatic—to restore compliance. Traditional arms control measures are not effective against biology. Using them, we could prove neither non-compliance nor compliance.

Traditional arms control measures, in fact, applied to biological activities yield no benefit and actually do great harm. Declarations and investigations called for under the draft Protocol at industrial plants, scientific labs, universities, and defense facilities would have revealed trade secrets and sensitive bio-defense information. The United States invests over a billion dollars annually on bio-defense. The U.S. pharmaceutical and biotech industry leads the world; each year, U.S. industry produces more than 50% of the new medicines created. It costs an average of $802 million to bring a new product to market and takes between 12–15 years to do so. Such disclosures, intentionally or inadvertently, also could result in putting the men and women in uniform at increased risk to biological weapons attacks. Protective devices and treatments could be compromised.

The draft Protocol would also have put in jeopardy effective export control regimes. Countries such as Iran, Iraq, and Cuba have fought the hardest for free access to the technology, knowledge, and equipment necessary to pursue biological weapons. Their argument was simple: as States Parties to the BWC they should be allowed free trade in all biological materials. These countries sought to dismantle effective export control regimes such as the Australia Group.[1] They

1. The Australia Group consists of thirty-three countries that coordinate export control policies.

argued that export controls should not be applied to BWC States Parties. The problem is that some BWC States Parties are pursuing biological warfare programs and it is no coincidence that these countries are also the ones pressing for access to sensitive technology. This "Trojan Horse" approach was not combated effectively by the draft Protocol. The result was a so-called "Cooperation Committee" whose job would have been to promote scientific and technological exchanges. The Cooperation Committee was touted as a way to appease Iran and Cuba. We viewed it as dangerous, harmful, and unnecessary. Protecting existing export control regimes is another important reason for the United States to reject the draft Protocol.

A lot of pressure was put on the United States to continue to support the draft Protocol simply because it was the result of seven years of hard negotiations. Several states urged our support by telling us that the draft Protocol was "better than nothing." Well, this was simply not sufficient to win U.S. support. We carefully studied the draft Protocol and found it to be a least common denominator compromise that, in our view, was worse than nothing.

Let me tell you something else about the draft Protocol. Several nations came to the United States privately and thanked us for rejecting the Protocol, which in their view was seriously flawed but for them was untouchable for political reasons. I know the United States did the right thing in rejecting the draft Protocol. The time for "better than nothing" proposals is over. It is time for us to work together to address the BW threat. . . .

U.S. Policy Toward the BWC

There has been confusion about America's policy toward the Biological Weapons Convention. . . . I want to discuss this policy.

The world must end its silent acquiescence to illicit biological weapons programs. The United States seeks to put maximum political pressure on proliferators by naming state parties that are violators of the BWC. We believe it is critical to put on notice such states that choose to ignore the norms of civilized society and pursue biological weapons.

These states must realize that their efforts to develop these terrible weapons will not go unnoticed. Our President has set a standard all should meet: tell the truth; speak out; be clear. Advice worth following, especially when it comes to biological weapons.

The United States Should Withdraw from the BWC

Rather than hope that the United Nations will produce a better protocol, the United States ought to realize that the Biological Weapons Convention is a proven failure—having already induced the creation of massive stockpiles of sophisticated biowar agents by the Soviet Union, stockpiles that remain available for terrorists or anyone else who can get hold of them. . . . The BWC was a well-intentioned mistake by people who mistook peace agreements for peace itself.

Article XIII, section 2, of the BWC authorizes signatories to withdraw from the treaty, after giving three months notice, if "extraordinary events, related to the subject matter of the Convention, have jeopardized the supreme interests of its country." The creation of what is unquestionably the largest and worst germ warfare industry in history—the [Soviet Union's] Biopreparat—as a direct result of the BWC was certainly "extraordinary," and the Biopreparat's products continue to jeopardize the "supreme interests" of the United States. Who knows what other countries have followed the Soviet lead and today are producing biowar weapons because the BWC guarantees that the United States can't fight fire with fire?

If the Bush administration's priority is to protect the American people from biological warfare, it must be willing to take decisive action and withdraw from the BWC, even if it means incurring the wrath of "the international community."

Dave Kopel and Glenn Reynolds, *National Review Online*, September 6, 2001.

Now concerning the Ad Hoc Group, the negotiating body for the BWC Protocol, the raison d'etre of the Ad Hoc Group has been to see that a draft Protocol based on traditional arms control measures comes into force. Many nations want to use the Ad Hoc Group to revive the draft Protocol at a later date or negotiate a new agreement based on traditional measures. Having determined that the traditional measures are not effective on biology and that those measures would put national security information and confidential business information at risk, the United States said there was no longer a need for the Ad Hoc Group. Our objections to the Protocol and those traditional measures on which it is based are real. We need to find a way to move beyond this debate and focus on what counts: a strengthened commitment to combat the biological weapons threat.

My speech up to this point may have led some to question what can be done to combat that threat. Well, I have good news. The United States last fall [of 2001] proposed several important measures to combat the BW threat, through means that would be far more effective than the draft Protocol. In the past year great progress has been made to combat the threat posed by biological weapons. National, bilateral, and multilateral efforts have made it more difficult for those pursuing biological weapons to obtain the necessary ingredients and made it easier to detect and counter any attack.

Since the [2001] anthrax attacks . . . the United States has enacted two new laws to improve our ability to combat the threat.

- The USA Patriot Act, signed on October 2001, provides national security and federal law enforcement officials with the necessary tools and resources to better counter terrorist activities.
- In June 2002, the Public Health Security and Bio-terrorist Preparedness and Response Act was adopted, which strengthens and enhances national bio-defense activities. The United States has placed great emphasis on working multilaterally and with likeminded groups to combat the BW threat.
- At the G-8 Summit in June [2002], members announced the "G-8 Global Partnership Against the Spread of Weapons and Materials of Mass Destruction." The United States pledged $10 billion toward this effort and urged other G-8 states to donate $10 billion over 10 years, with the aim of enhancing projects underway in the former Soviet Union, including projects dedicated toward reducing BW proliferation.
- In May 2002, World Health Organization members

agreed to strengthen health surveillance systems to detect any possible BW attack and improve international responses to stop any resultant outbreak.

- Also in May 2002, NATO's Defense Group on Proliferation set forth a number of initiatives to improve NATO's ability to combat and counter any biological weapons attack, including stockpiling medicines and protective equipment.
- In June 2002, Australia Group members adopted tougher export measures to control more effectively items that could be used to produce biological weapons, including adding controls on the transfer of information and knowledge that could aid BW proliferation.

The United States is committed to combating the BW threat. We will do so where we can and when we can. Recent efforts illustrate the U.S. commitment to combat the threat. Our other initiatives are underway in other effective forums. . . .

In conclusion, I would like to point out that the approaches of Japan and the United States to combating the threat posed by biological weapons are actually quite similar, and our goal of stopping the spread of weapons of mass destruction is the same. The Aum Shinrikyo sarin attack in Japan and the anthrax attacks in the United States have made both of our nations painfully aware that biological and chemical weapons can be used against us at any time. And the tragic events of September 11 showed us that terrorist groups will use any means at their disposal to strike against innocent targets. We must not allow biological weapons to become part of their arsenal.

Given the unique challenges involved in regulating biological agents and detecting their misuse, we must remain creative, vigilant and forward-looking in combating the BW threat. And we will remain steadfast in rejecting proposals that do not address the BW problem in a realistic manner but are simply the product of bureaucratic compromise. As the Japanese proverb goes, "Vision without action is a daydream. Action without vision is a nightmare."

> *"If a non-nuclear state used a biological weapon against the United States, it should be on notice that it could pay a heavy nuclear price."*

Nuclear Deterrence Can Prevent Biological Warfare

David G. Gompert

David G. Gompert is vice president of the Rand Corporation in Santa Monica, Calfornia, where he runs the National Security Research Division. In the following viewpoint, based on ideas he developed with Rand colleagues Dean Wilening and Kenneth Watman, he argues that the United States should make an explicit declaration that it is prepared to use nuclear arms against any nation that attacks America with biological weapons. Such a policy of nuclear deterrence could prevent the United States from ever being victimized by biological warfare, he contends.

As you read, consider the following questions:

1. Why is Gompert more concerned about biological weapons than about chemical weapons?
2. How does Gompert respond to the idea that the United States should rely on conventional weapon superiority to deter nations from using biological weapons?
3. Why should the United States make its position on using nuclear weapons explicit instead of ambiguous, according to Gompert?

David G. Gompert, "Sharpen the Fear," *Bulletin of the Atomic Scientists*, January/February 2000, pp. 22–23, 76–77. Copyright © 2000 by the Educational Foundation for Nuclear Science, www.thebulletin.org; a one-year subscription is $28. Reproduced by permission.

Although nuclear arms control negotiations have stalled in recent years, U.S. and Russian nuclear arsenals have been greatly reduced. That suggests that nuclear weapons now have—and will continue to have—a reduced role in world affairs. That is surely a good thing. But precisely what that role will be remains unclear.

Many arms control enthusiasts . . . believe that a declaratory policy of "no-first-use" of nuclear weapons—pledging never to use nuclear weapons except in retaliation against a nuclear attack—is a critical step in assuring nuclear peace.

But that would be a risky strategy. Attempting to lower the danger of nuclear violence through no-first-use would weaken the fear that nuclear weapons produce. If that fear helps prevent mass casualties from new and comparably dreadful weapons, we may not want to nullify it.

The Cold War and After

We have some experience with the fear of nuclear war. During the Cold War, it was used by the United States to engender caution and to produce stability. Had it not been for that fear, the twentieth century might have had three world wars instead of two.

The nuclear standoff—parity between arsenals large enough to assure mutual destruction—negated the nuclear threat and thus the likelihood of nuclear war. But simultaneously, the United States negated that negation by threatening to use nuclear weapons to block aggression by conventional Soviet forces. Featuring for their way of life, Americans risked nuclear war to buttress the status quo.

But the world has been transformed. The American way of life is no longer threatened; rather, it is on the march. Because the main current of change—globalization—promotes its interests and ideals, the United States no longer seeks to freeze the international situation. U.S. technological and conventional military capabilities instill confidence in means other than nuclear weapons to thwart conventional aggression.

Should the United States therefore embrace no-first-use, the opposite of the U.S. Cold War doctrine on the use of nuclear weapons? Should it disengage nuclear weapons altogether from international security and military strategy, relying on them solely to deter nuclear war? Is this human-kind's chance to eradicate nuclear fear, even if the weapons themselves cannot be eradicated?

Regrettably, the answer is no.

Although the threat of a nuclear response to a conventional attack is no longer crucial to U.S. strategy, the United States still needs nuclear weapons to deter a nuclear attack. But it must also, I believe, present a threat of nuclear retaliation to deter a biological attack, which could be as deadly, and which might not be deterred by the threat of U.S. conventional retaliation.

In this century, the United States should aim to reduce the importance and attractiveness of nuclear weapons and it should delegitimize their use in response to conventional threats. But it must also sharpen nuclear deterrence against biological weapons. The United States could do this by stating that it would use nuclear weapons only in retaliation for attacks with weapons of mass destruction (WMD).

Such a policy of no-first-use of weapons of mass destruction would better support U.S. and international security than either a policy of no-first-use of nuclear weapons or the current official policy, which in its ambiguity rules out nothing. . . .

Redefining Threats

With its technological lead, its growing conventional military superiority, the absence of a mortal enemy, its stature in other forms of power, and its confidence in the face of change, the United States could decouple nuclear weapons from its military strategy and foreign policy without endangering the nation. But before redefining the purpose of nuclear weapons, we must ask if there are any emerging non-nuclear threats that warrant the threat, or the option, of a nuclear response.

Like most technologies, dangerous or benign, biochemical technology is spreading as the global economy integrates. Consequently, U.S. forces, U.S. allies, and eventually U.S. citizens will be vulnerable to attack with biological and chemical weapons delivered by long-range missiles or by clandestine means.

Of the two types, chemical and biological, the latter

weapons present the greater danger of casualties on a nuclear scale. Ten kilograms of anthrax is at least as deadly as a 10-kilogram nuclear explosive, and it is cheaper, easier to assemble, and more portable.

While chemical weapons are more likely to be used to disrupt U.S. military operations, biological weapons pose terrible and lingering dangers to the general population, much like strategic nuclear weapons.

The most immediate concern is that rogue states, lacking other options, might threaten to use biological weapons against U.S. troops in a local war. The United States can partly neutralize this threat by exploiting information technology—dispersing its forces and striking accurately from afar. But determined enemies will then resort to longer-range means to threaten U.S. forces, allies, and territory.

Try as it might to stop the spread of these weapons, the United States must prepare to prevent or defend against their use. But defense alone, with anti-missile and counterforce weapons, cannot make American forces and citizens entirely safe from lethal biological agents. Deterrence is crucial.

A Conventional Reprisal Is Not Enough

A common argument is that U.S. conventional military superiority—the ability to render an adversary defenseless—should suffice to deter the use of weapons of mass destruction. However, an enemy may already be receiving the full brunt of U.S. conventional strikes when it opts to threaten biological attack. Indeed, the most plausible reason why a rogue state would threaten to use weapons of mass destruction is that the United States has already unleashed its conventional might to defeat local aggression.

Given that, the threat of U.S. conventional reprisal presumably would be ineffective. And because the United States has forsworn biological and chemical weapons, deterrence could depend critically on the threat to retaliate with nuclear weapons. That, of course, would be contradicted by a nuclear no-first-use policy.

The countries whose WMD programs most worry the United States are rogue states such as Iraq, North Korea, and Iran. Because the aim of such states is to deter a U.S.

conventional attack, it follows that an American pledge not to use nuclear weapons first, even if they had faith in it, would not diminish their interest in nuclear weapons.

Presumably rogue states already know that using nuclear weapons against U.S. interests could trigger U.S. nuclear retaliation. However, they may view biological weapons as more usable, more credible, and less risky, not to mention easier to obtain or make. A U.S. pledge not to use nuclear weapons first would make them even more eager to acquire—and less hesitant to brandish and use—biological weapons.

The Multilateral Deterrence Option

All governments now have a practical reason for opposing weapons of mass destruction: transnational terrorism.

The time may be ripe for America to join other nuclear weapons states in a joint policy: to refrain from use of any weapon of mass destruction unless another state or terrorist network used such a weapon first or is unambiguously about to do so. The form of retaliation against use of chemical or biological weapons would not necessarily be in kind. Nuclear weapons might be unleashed against a state that used biological weapons first.

This bold step would make the permanent members of the UN Security Council—each a nuclear power—de facto partners in acting together against any entity that thought the use of chemical, biological, or nuclear weapons would give it some advantage.

Hans Binnendijk and James Goodby, *Christian Science Monitor*, May 30, 2002.

While it is possible to imagine a biological attack that would not warrant a nuclear response, this is no reason to discard the option of a nuclear response against any and all possible biological attacks.

When thousands of Soviet nuclear weapons were poised to strike, the first use of nuclear weapons by the United States risked a general nuclear cataclysm. In contrast, U.S. nuclear retaliation for a biological attack by a rogue state would risk, at worst, another WMD attack—awful to be sure, but worth the risk in order to deter biological use in the first place.

More likely, having proven its resolve with a presumably selective nuclear detonation, the United States would deter further escalation and prevail. In any case, being prepared to respond to an attack by weapons of mass destruction with nuclear weapons—and by saying so—the United States would be less likely to have to do so.

Of course, U.S. nuclear retaliation for a biological attack would be a grave, world-changing event. But it would not imperil the nation and its global interests, let alone human viability. And it would make it less likely that any weapon of mass destruction—at least a biological or nuclear one—would ever be used again, and certainly not against the United States.

A Fresh Idea

The strongest argument for a nuclear no-first-use pledge during the Cold War was that it could have saved the United States from nuclear hell. The strongest argument against such a pledge was that it could have condemned the United States to a communist hell.

Now that the Soviet Union is gone, neither argument is persuasive. Concepts saved in the attic from a different time, a different world, are not helpful. Both nuclear first-use and nuclear no-first-use are out of date. A fresh idea is needed.

During the Cold War, the United States would not exclude a nuclear response to any aggression. It was motivated by both a general concern, the Soviet menace, and a specific concern, a tank attack on West Germany. The former was the context and the latter was the sharp focal point of U.S. first-use doctrine. It was surely the specific prospect that the United States might resort to nuclear weapons if war broke out in Europe that got the Kremlin's attention.

Now the United States wants rogue states to think that the use of biological weapons could cause a disproportionate response; it wants them to feel this fear quite sharply. To the extent that the United States fails to pinpoint this in defining the purpose of nuclear weapons, that fear will be dull and its utility will be lost.

The Problem with Ambiguity

Current U.S. policy regarding the use of nuclear weapons is not substantially different from its general Cold War policy. The United States maintains ambiguity about the circumstances under which it would resort to nuclear weapons. Despite growing and enduring U.S. conventional military superiority, even a nuclear response to conventional attack is not excluded.

And yet, so unreal is the thought that the United States would use nuclear weapons in response to conventional attack that the current open-ended policy actually dulls deterrence. As long as the United States refuses to rule out an option that is now patently incredible (nuclear retaliation for conventional aggression), it undermines the credibility of an option that could prove crucial (nuclear retaliation for biological attack). Ambiguity is sometimes useful. But in the new era, it does more harm than good.

The United States should explicitly warn that it might respond with a weapon of mass destruction—nuclear weapons—to an attack by a weapon of mass destruction against U.S. interests. (Chemical weapons could be included, although it could be made clear that the greater concern is biological weapons.)

But that is not enough. To sharpen the fear to a finer point, the United States should also say that it foresees no need to use nuclear weapons except in response to attacks by weapons of mass destruction.

A declaratory policy along these lines would reinforce deterrence by erasing the incredible aspect of current policy—that is, nuclear response to conventional aggression. And it would bolster the taboo against first use of any weapon of mass destruction—a taboo that today appears too weak for comfort.

In past efforts to stem the spread of nuclear weapons, the United States has said, in effect, that it would not use nuclear weapons against states that forswear them. But what if a state acquired biological weapons which can kill Americans no less effectively than nuclear explosives? What if the state used them?

In light of this danger, the United States should retract its pledge not to use nuclear weapons against any non-nuclear states. If a non-nuclear state used a biological weapon against the United States, it should be on notice that it could pay a heavy nuclear price. . . .

Looking to the Future

One hopes the time will come when nuclear weapons can be retired. With its natural and durable advantages, the United States should want this as much as any country. Nuclear weapons may be hard to outlaw, but the world may eventually outlive or outgrow the nuclear era. Perhaps the information age, with its emphasis on precision weapons, can reduce the scale of deadly conflict. If, as well, the new age blesses free-market democracies with superior power, the world may become increasingly safe and the need to rely on nuclear weapons to keep it safe may fade away.

We are not there yet. Rogue states are on the ropes, but they can hang on and do great harm if they acquire weapons of mass destruction. By concentrating nuclear deterrence on this particular problem, by creating a sharp fear, and by limiting the purpose of nuclear weapons to retaliation for attacks by weapons of mass destruction, the United States may help move the world a step closer to a world in which none of these horrible weapons would ever again be used.

"*Nuclear deterrence is ill-suited to protecting the United States and its interests against . . . biological attacks.*"

Nuclear Deterrence Should Not Be Used to Prevent Biological Warfare

Thomas Graham Jr.

Thomas Graham Jr., a former senior U.S. diplomat, is the president of the Lawyers Alliance for World Security. In the following viewpoint, he takes issue with the idea that the United States should explicitly threaten the use of nuclear arms against any nation that attempts to attack it using biological weapons. The United States has pledged not to use nuclear weapons against non-nuclear states who have signed the Nuclear Non-Proliferation Treaty (NPT); Graham argues that to make an exception in the case of a biological weapons attack would undermine efforts against nuclear proliferation by encouraging non-nuclear states that fear biological weapons to develop nuclear arms. The United States should instead utilize its significant conventional military assets to deter other nations from waging biological warfare, he concludes.

As you read, consider the following questions:

1. How might an American policy of nuclear retaliation against a biological attack undermine the global effort against nuclear proliferation, according to Graham?
2. How does nuclear proliferation work against America's security interests, in the author's opinion?

R ecent suggestions that the United States should change
its defense policy to explicitly deter chemical or biological weapons attacks with nuclear weapons are misguided
and potentially dangerous. Nuclear deterrence is ill-suited
to protecting the United States and its interests against
chemical or biological attacks and to "employ" it in this fashion would make the spread of nuclear weapons much more
likely. We can deter and respond to chemical and biological
weapons in a manner fully protective of our national security; we cannot assure our national security in a world armed
to the teeth with nuclear weapons.

As the 1997 report by the U.S. National Academy of Sciences, "The Future of U.S. Nuclear Weapons Policy," sets
forth, the appropriate role of nuclear weapons in the post–
Cold War world is "core deterrence," that is deterring the
use of nuclear weapons by others. Defining the role of U.S.
nuclear weapons in this way strengthens the Nuclear Non-
Proliferation Treaty (NPT) regime and sets the stage for
further efforts to reduce the danger posed by the overarma-
ment of the Cold War. . . .

The United States's 1978 pledge (made at the first United
Nations Special Session on Disarmament) not to use or
threaten to use nuclear weapons against non-nuclear
weapon states party to the NPT unless they attack the
United States in alliance with a nuclear weapon state is an
important element of the NPT regime. There is no exception in this commitment for chemical or biological weapons.
Numerous non-nuclear weapon states made their decision
to join the NPT after this commitment was announced.
This commitment (referred to as a negative security assurance) was reaffirmed in April 1995 in association with other
nuclear weapon states in the context of the 1995 NPT Review and Extension Conference. Without it, the indefinite
extension of the NPT might not have taken place and the
then 178 (now 185) state parties to the NPT agreed to its indefinite extension relying on this reaffirmation.

To announce that a role for U.S. nuclear weapons is to deter chemical and biological weapons in the hands of a non-
nuclear weapon state—in other words to threaten to retaliate
with nuclear weapons if chemical or biological weapons are

Misplaced Faith in Nuclear Deterrence

Sad to say, the Cold War lives on in the minds of those who cannot let go the fears, beliefs and the enmities born of the nuclear age. What better illustration of misplaced faith in nuclear deterrence than the persistent belief that retaliation with nuclear weapons is a legitimate and appropriate response to post Cold War threats posed by biological and chemical weapons of mass destruction as well as by conventional weapons, and not just nuclear weapons. What could possibly justify our resort to the very means we properly abhor and condemn? Who can imagine our joining in shattering the precedent of non-use that has held for over 50 years? Would we hold an entire society accountable for the decision of a single demented leader? How would the physical effects of the nuclear explosion be contained, not to mention the political and moral consequences? . . . It is wrong in every aspect. It is wrong politically. It makes no sense militarily. And morally, in my view, it is indefensible.

Lee Butler, *Disarmament Times*, April 1998.

---

used against the United States by such a state—would be a violation of this negative security assurance, jeopardizing the NPT regime. Disavowal of the U.S. NPT-related negative security assurance would be perceived by many nations as an act of bad faith with respect to our nuclear arms control and disarmament obligations under Article VI of the NPT. Further if the United States were to argue, for example, that we need nuclear weapons to offset Iraq's biological weapons why couldn't Iran (or any other state) make the same argument. . . . [Giving] U.S. nuclear weapons the explicit role of deterring chemical and biological weapons would simply be an invitation to nuclear weapon proliferation. . . . It is the NPT regime which has prompted the vast majority of the world's nations not to build nuclear weapons. If the United States does not live up to the bargain it made in the context of NPT extension, the half-dozen nuclear proliferation threats of today could become many more tomorrow.

Conventional Power

The way to deal with threats of the use of chemical and biological weapons is with the overwhelming conventional power of the United States. The United States should ensure that in the future any state that resorts to chemical or biological weapons pays an unbearable price. However, to threaten retaliation with nuclear weapons would only encourage countries who are threatened by chemical or biological weapons to seek their own nuclear weapon capability. Were countries to begin to do this, the NPT would fail and our massive conventional superiority would be neutralized by the widespread proliferation of nuclear weapons. The United States should do everything it can to support and enhance the NPT regime which is the cornerstone of international security and maintain the long standing firebreak between nuclear weapons and chemical and biological weapons. If nuclear deterrence is somewhat underemployed, let it remain so. The less dependent we are on nuclear weapons for our defense the more secure we will be.

"It is difficult to find anyone who knows personally the horrors of epidemic smallpox and who favors retaining the virus."

All Known Stocks of the Smallpox Virus Should Be Destroyed

Donald A. Henderson and Frank Fenner

Donald A. Henderson led the World Health Organization's Global Smallpox Eradication Program that successfully eliminated all natural outbreaks of the disease and left the world with only two known stocks of the smallpox virus, one in the United States and the other in the Soviet Union (later Russia). In 1999 and again in 2002, both the United States and the World Health Organization postponed the scheduled destruction of these last repositories. In the following viewpoint, published in 2001, Henderson and coauthor Frank Fenner of the John Curtin School of Medical Research at Australian National University call for the destruction of all known stocks of the smallpox virus. They argue that retaining stocks for research is unlikely to yield practical results and is not worth the risk of some nation or group attempting to use smallpox as a biological weapon.

As you read, consider the following questions:
1. What are the two primary research objectives that might justify retaining the smallpox virus, according to Henderson and Fenner?
2. Why would a smallpox antiviral drug be impractical, according to the authors?

Donald A. Henderson and Frank Fenner, "Recent Events and Observations Pertaining to Smallpox Virus Destruction in 2002," *Clinical Infectious Diseases*, October 1, 2001, pp. 1057–59. Copyright © 2001 by the Infectious Disease Society of America. Reproduced by permission.

[In 1999] the 52d World Health Assembly reaffirmed the decision of previous assemblies that the remaining stocks of variola [smallpox] virus should be destroyed. However, it authorized "temporary retention up to [but] not later than 2002 and subject to annual review by the World Health Assembly." It provided for the creation of an expert group to oversee an interim research program and to assure the adequacy of containment measures taken by the laboratories. Since that time, important progress has been made, and other considerations have emerged as scientists and policy makers have given further thought to the potential outcomes of present research as they pertain to considerations of public health and national security.

This summary communication addresses the most pertinent of these considerations and indicates why we continue to believe that it is most important to adhere to the provisions and deadline established by the 1999 Assembly.

At the first meeting of the expert group (in December 1999), two research objectives were identified as the primary reasons for retaining variola virus: (1) the possible development of a more attenuated, less reactogenic smallpox vaccine, and (2) the possible development of an antiviral drug that could be used in treatment of patients with smallpox. An ancillary but important initiative was to evaluate again the possibility of establishing a functional variola virus/monkey model to facilitate the two research objectives.

A More Attenuated Vaccine

In the United States, a vaccine strain that would be as effective as the New York Board of Health (NYBOH) strain but that would be less prone to induce complications was originally seen as a desirable objective. In June 2000, an interagency meeting of government scientists was convened at the Centers for Disease Control and Prevention to determine the possibility of further evaluating currently available attenuated strains of vaccinia. . . .

The group recognized that if smallpox were to be released, the threat of its spreading widely was of paramount concern. Existing vaccine strains . . . have been shown, in the circumstances of a natural challenge, to provide solid protection to almost all who received them, even when administered 2–3 days after exposure. Such an assurance of efficacy would be impossible to provide for *any* experimental vaccine simply because challenge in natural circumstances is no longer possible. Thus, a decision was made to procure additional NYBOH vaccine for the US national reserve. This conclusion effectively forecloses the rationale for further research on modified vaccines. Thus, it would seem appropriate that future research efforts pertaining to vaccination be directed toward mitigating the possible effects of adverse reactions to vaccinia through use of such as antivaccinial drugs or mono-clonal antibodies.

An Antiviral Drug

As further mature consideration has been given to the possibility of developing an antiviral drug, several difficult and practical considerations have arisen that, taken together, question both the feasibility and wisdom of pursuing this strategy.

First is the question of cost for development and licensure of a new antiviral entity. Pharmaceutical manufacturers estimate that it costs in excess of $500 million and some 8–10 years of research and development to bring to market a new antimicrobial product. No government has yet [as of 2001] signaled its willingness to make an investment of this magnitude for development of a new antiviral agent and quite possibly to expend substantially more than that amount of money again in providing a reasonably sized stockpile for possible use. Further funds would need to be set aside for replenishment of supplies as they deteriorated over time.

Second is the question of how much confidence either clinicians or public health professionals could have in using, under emergency conditions, an experimental drug either to treat patients after rash has emerged or to prevent disease among those who might have been exposed and possibly infected. However effective such a product might appear to be in tissue culture or in experiments with monkeys (a surrogate host) infected with monkeypox virus (a surrogate virus), no one could be confident that it would be effective in humans. The only reliable test would be the successful treatment of humans infected with variola virus, and that would be impossible except under epidemic circumstances. Perhaps somewhat more confidence in a new drug would accrue were there a variola/monkey model, but efforts to identify a satisfactory model have continued to meet with no success.

The Horrors of Smallpox

It is difficult to find anyone who knows personally the horrors of epidemic smallpox and who favors retaining the virus. The disease kills 30 percent; there is no treatment. Those who survive are left severely pock-marked, and some are blinded. It is no wonder that before its eradication in 1979, smallpox was the most feared of all the pestilential diseases.

Donald A. Henderson, *Biodefense Quarterly*, June 1999.

Third are the practical limitations, from a clinical and public health perspective, for use of an antiviral agent even if one were available. A therapeutic drug would be useful for treatment of some patients during the first and possibly second wave of cases. By then, the more certain and practicable strategy of prevention through vaccination would take precedence over treatment and would certainly be given preference in use of resources.

To use an antiviral agent as a prophylactic—that is, to prevent development of smallpox among those potentially exposed—would pose a staggering task to the most sophisticated and well-staffed public health system. Even assuming the need for only one dose of a drug daily, the practical logistics of distributing sufficient drugs to cover the large numbers of persons potentially exposed, to provide sufficient supervision to assure that such drugs were actually taken daily, and to pursue such a regimen throughout the weeks, if not months, that cases might be expected to occur would tax all resources. Clearly, vaccination has to be the primary defense. It is inexpensive; large-scale programs can be organized rapidly; and, with a single inoculation, it provides a level of protection that would be unlikely to be achieved with a drug, whenever or however administered.

An antiviral drug might be useful in preventing disease in immune-compromised persons who would be at risk of occurrence of progressive vaccinia, if vaccinated. However, it would seem to us to make more sense to focus research efforts on the development of an anti-*vaccinial* drug that could be used to treat cases of progressive vaccinia should they occur. Such a drug could be much more fully evaluated in animal studies, thus providing a high level of confidence that it would be effective when circumstances called for its use. Such research would not require retention of variola virus.

Genetically Engineered Viruses

Concern about the possible development of more-virulent recombinant strains of variola has arisen, stemming from Australian studies showing that an ectromelia-IL4 recombinant kills mice that are naturally resistant to the virus and also kills those mice who have been vaccinated. All manner of other hypothetical scenarios can be and have been imagined. Some have argued that the recombinant threat alone should be reason enough for retaining variola virus strains. Superficially, this might seem prudent, but the implications to us suggest otherwise. There might be logic in a broad-based research program to explore the range of possible alterations in the genome that might be induced and so better define the nature of the threat. However, not only would such experiments be in direct violation of the Biologic and Toxin Weapons Convention, but they might, at the same time, define a whole new array of bioweapons, more awesome than any now known. And, predictably, these would not be kept secret for very long. Thus, it seems to us that there is a stronger argument than ever for bringing to bear all possible political and moral suasion to persuade countries and laboratories to destroy existing stocks of smallpox virus and to cease all research on variola virus itself. Nothing can guarantee that this will prevent an international catastrophe, but it would serve to mitigate the likelihood of its occurrence.

Smallpox Virus in Other Laboratories

Finally, notice should be taken of the press's frequent allusions to the fact that destruction of the virus is being postponed because of recent reports that laboratories other than those in Atlanta, the United States, and Novosibirsk, Russian Federation, might have retained smallpox virus. The question of whether other laboratories might or might not have surreptitiously retained strains of smallpox has not been nor should it now be a consideration in deciding whether or not the Assembly asks all countries to destroy their stocks of smallpox virus. The World Health Organization Expert Committee on Orthopoxvirus Infections recognized from its earliest meetings that there was no way that anyone could ever verify that each and every country had destroyed its stock of virus. To think otherwise would be naïve. To the Committee, it seemed reasonable then, and seems as reasonable now, to assume that the risk of a smallpox virus release would be *diminished* were the World Health Assembly to call on each country to destroy its stocks of smallpox virus and to state that any person, laboratory, or country found to have virus after date x would be guilty of a crime against humanity. This approach would be entirely consonant with activities now contemplated under the broader Biological Weapons Convention to abolish research on and production of offensive biological weapons.

The logic and importance of actions to destroy all remaining stocks of variola virus . . . seem to us to be . . . compelling.

> *"Destroying existing [smallpox virus] supplies might put the public health community at a critical disadvantage . . . in the event of a biological attack."*

Known Stocks of the Smallpox Virus Should Be Retained for Research

Joshua Micah Marshall

Thanks to an international eradication campaign, the only known stocks of the smallpox virus are contained in facilities in the United States and Russia. Some have called for these to be destroyed to prevent their accidental or intentional release. In the following viewpoint, political writer Joshua Micah Marshall criticizes this proposal and rejects the claims of one of the plan's proponents, Donald A. Henderson. Marshall writes that many public health experts have concluded that nations other than the United States and Russia may be hiding smallpox stocks, which they could one day use to infect the American population during a terrorist attack or war. He contends that the United States should retain its stores of the deadly virus to help scientists discover and improve on smallpox vaccinations and treatments that could be used in the event of such an attack.

As you read, consider the following questions:
1. What, in Marshall's opinion, is the key question in the debate over whether to destroy smallpox virus stocks?
2. What flaws exist in the established smallpox vaccine, according to the author?

W hen Secretary of Health and Human Services Tommy Thompson announced that he was appointing Dr. Donald A. Henderson as his bioterrorism czar earlier this month [November 2001], you could almost hear the collective sigh of relief. After all, who better to defend the country against biological attack than Henderson, the grand old man of smallpox eradication, who led the successful World Health Organization (WHO) effort to wipe out the disease in the 1960s and 1970s? *The Boston Globe* described Henderson as "one of the giants in public health"; Thompson himself boasted that Henderson's appointment completed a "scientific dream team" and noted that "his distinguished record speaks for itself."

Which is true enough, insofar as it goes. The problem is that Henderson's efforts didn't stop with the eradication of smallpox in nature. For years now Henderson has also been bent on eradicating smallpox in the lab, as the leading advocate of destroying the last-known government stocks of the virus—an irreversible step that most experts believe would have prevented medical advances critical to defending against a smallpox attack. "Destroying the smallpox virus would have been the single largest mistake that I can think of as far as counterterrorism or counterproliferation is concerned," says Al Zelicoff, a physician and senior scientist at the Center for National Security and Arms Control at Sandia National Laboratories. In other words, before assuming his new role as director of the Office of Public Health Preparedness, Henderson spent the better part of the last decade pushing an agenda that would have left the country much less prepared for a terrorist attack on public health.

Smallpox Proliferation Concerns

A decade ago most policymakers and research scientists agreed that the last two WHO-approved laboratory stocks of smallpox virus—one at the Centers for Disease Control and Prevention (CDC) in Atlanta, and another at the Vektor Institute in Siberia—should eventually be destroyed. But destroying them only made sense if they *really were* the only two supplies left. Otherwise, destroying existing supplies might put the public health community at a critical disadvantage in developing new smallpox vaccines and antiviral medications in the event of a biological attack. What if other countries were hiding additional, illicit stocks of smallpox virus in their biological weapons arsenals?

And, over the course of the 1990s, evidence mounted that indeed they were. Not only did it become clear that the former Soviet Union (and later Russia) had stockpiled large quantities of smallpox, but there were clear—though by no means conclusive—signs that countries such as North Korea might have acquired supplies as well. Over time, that information brought most pro-destruction advocates over to the pro-retention side.

But not Donald Henderson. For years Henderson either disputed or disparaged the growing evidence of smallpox proliferation, making himself a thorn in the sides of defense and counterterrorism experts who believed smallpox constituted a serious bioterrorism threat. When evidence of proliferation grew overwhelming in the late 1990s, Henderson shifted gears and began arguing that only by destroying our own supply of smallpox could the United States garner the moral authority to persuade countries like Russia or North Korea to do the same. Retaining the virus, Henderson wrote in 1999, "would provide the argument for various countries to obtain the smallpox virus for their own studies. Possibly, the smallpox virus could be disseminated to many laboratories, including ones in Iraq and North Korea." Even today he ridicules the national security arguments for holding onto America's supplies of the virus. "There's a great desire on the part of [the Department of Defense] to justify retaining the smallpox virus," he told *Science* magazine just last month [October 2002]. "And that's what it all boils down to."

Vaccine Research

The key question in the smallpox-retention debate is whether having stores of the virus on hand would aid the development of improved vaccines and critical antiviral medications. "It became clear to me [in the course of research conducted in the mid-1990s] that loss of the virus would eliminate opportunities to develop new drugs," says David Franz, former commander of the U.S. Army Medical Re-

search Institute of Infectious Diseases (USAMRIID). For his part, Henderson (who declined to be interviewed for this article) has argued that the established smallpox vaccine is sufficient to defend against a possible bioterrorism-related smallpox outbreak, and that research on new drugs and vaccines would be either unworkable or prohibitively costly.

But others point out that the established vaccine suffers from two major flaws: It can prove fatal to those with suppressed immune systems and, in the case of a bioterrorist attack, would provide immunity to those infected only if they were vaccinated within days of exposure. "We need antiviral drugs as well," says Zelicoff, "for the people who can't take the vaccine . . . and those who don't get it in time."

Too Valuable to Be Destroyed

The symbolism of destroying the remaining stocks of smallpox virus is highly unlikely to influence anyone contemplating biological warfare or terrorism. The tenuous hope that it might exert such influence in no way outweighs the loss of a genome that has evolved to interact more specifically with human defense mechanisms than any other. It encodes too many unique reagents to warrant destruction.

Wolfgang K. Joklik, *The Scientist*, December 9, 1996.

The current smallpox vaccine is a "live virus" vaccine. That means when you get inoculated, you are exposed to an actual virus—in this case, *vaccinia*, a close variant of the virus that causes cowpox, the bovine analog of smallpox. A person with a healthy immune system can fight off the disease and, in so doing, acquire an immunity to the far-deadlier smallpox virus. But in a person with a suppressed immune system, *vaccinia* can produce serious or even fatal illness. And that fact is far more important today than it was when Americans were last routinely inoculated because, over the past 30 years, the percentage of the population with suppressed immune systems has risen dramatically. AIDS patients, chemotherapy patients, and anyone with an organ transplant would find themselves among the millions of Americans unable to receive the vaccine. (It's even possible that people with immunosuppression could contract the *vaccinia* virus through

close contact with healthy people who had been recently in-oculated.) The best hope for the immunosuppressed popu-lation probably lies in high-tech antiviral drugs—the kind Henderson says we don't need.

Antiviral Drugs

Antivirals would likely also play a critical role in protecting the healthy population. Under current government plans, public health authorities would try to stamp out a bioterror-ism smallpox outbreak by initiating mass inoculations in the affected area. But the smallpox vaccine only offers protec-tion if it is administered within three to four days of expo-sure. Given smallpox's long incubation period, it's likely many individuals would have gone longer than three days since exposure once the first signs of an outbreak appeared. Preliminary research by scientists at USAMRIID suggests that antiviral drugs would be effective longer into the course of the illness. The same researchers also believe that antivi-ral drugs would be useful against genetically manipulated strains of smallpox that the *vaccinia*-based vaccine might be powerless to control.

When the destruction question was last debated inside the U.S. government in 1999, Henderson downplayed the pos-sibility that antiviral drug research would ever pan out or improve on the protection offered by the established vac-cine. In a 1999 editorial in *The Baltimore Sun*, he called de-veloping such new drugs neither "likely nor practical" and said it would be impossible to develop new treatments be-cause scientists would not be able to find an animal species on which such drugs could be accurately tested.

But subsequent research has belied both those predic-tions. Since 1999 researchers from USAMRIID working at the CDC have used the live smallpox virus to isolate twelve potential antiviral drugs that work against smallpox in lab experiments. "We've made a lot of progress toward develop-ing antiviral drugs working with the virus since 1999," says a senior Clinton administration official closely involved in the 1999 debate. "If we would have destroyed it then it would have stopped us dead in our tracks."

Moreover, last year a USAMRIID researcher, Dr. Peter

Jahrling, discovered and is now refining a so-called "animal model" for smallpox, which should facilitate precisely the sort of animal trials Henderson said would be impossible. As Sandia National Laboratories' Zelicoff puts it, "As a result of having the smallpox virus, we have done two things that experts said would be impossible . . . we've identified an entire series of antiviral drugs, [and] we now have a plausible animal model . . . that will enable us to test those drugs." No thanks to [Henderson].

Periodical Bibliography

The following articles have been selected to supplement the diverse views presented in this chapter.

Richard K. Betts "The New Threat of Mass Destruction," *Foreign Affairs*, January/February 1998.

Hans Binnendijk and James Goodby "Strengthen Nuclear Deterrence," *Christian Science Monitor*, May 30, 2002. www.csmonitor.com/2002/0530/p09 s01-coop.html.

George W. Christopher et al. "Biological Warfare: A Historical Perspective," *Journal of the American Medical Association*, August 6, 1997.

Michael Crowley "Combating Biological Weapons," *UN Chronicle*, June–August 2002.

Economist "A Viral-Bustup; Biological Weapons," December 8, 2001.

Wolfgang J. Joklik "The Remaining Smallpox Virus Stocks Are Too Valuable to Be Destroyed," *The Scientist*, December 9, 1996.

Deborah Mackenzie "Try Again, Mr. President: Bush's Ill-Conceived Bioweapons Proposals Won't Win Any Friends," *New Scientist*, November 10, 2001.

Robert S. McNamara and Thomas Graham "A Pretty Poor Posture for a Superpower," *Los Angeles Times*, March 13, 2002.

Elizabeth Olson "U.S. Calls for Global Action to Counter Germ Weapons," *New York Times*, November 20, 2001.

J.D. Reed "Virus Vanquisher: D.A. Henderson Led the Global Campaign to Eradicate Smallpox; Now He's Working Against Its Return," *Smithsonian*, February 2002.

Barbara H. Rosenberg "Allergic Reaction: Washington's Reponse to the BWC Protocol," *Arms Control Today*, July 2001.

Barbara H. Rosenberg and Milton Leitenberg "Who's Afraid of a Germ Warfare Treaty," *Los Angeles Times*, September 6, 2001.

Peter Slevin "U.S. Drops Bid to Strengthen Germ Warfare Accord," *Washington Post*, September 19, 2001.

Nicholas Stix "Media Manufacture Cloud of Suspicion over Hatfill," *Insight on the News*, August 12, 2002.

Richard Stone   "Down to the Wire on Bioweapons Talks,"
                 Science, July 20, 2001.

Jonathan B. Tucker   "Putting Teeth in the Biological Weapons
                      Convention," *Issues in Science and Technology*,
                      Spring 2002.

Mark Wheelis   "Biotechnology and Biochemical Weapons,"
                Nonproliferation Review, Spring 2002.

For Further Discussion

Chapter 1

1. In your opinion, how likely is it that the nightmare scenario described by Scott P. Layne and Michael H. Sommer will happen? Can you imagine other possible scenarios involving biological warfare that are more or less probable? Defend your answer with evidence from the viewpoints in this chapter.

2. Gregg Easterbrook argues that public perceptions of biological weapons have been shaped more by novels and movies rather than real events, which have been much less dramatic. After reading his viewpoint, do you agree or disagree with his criticism? Does the fact that a bioterrorist scenario is described in a science fiction novel make it a less worthy candidate of concern? Explain why or why not.

3. Americans are feeling anxious about a biological weapons attack in part because of the media, according to Henry I. Miller and Sherri Ferris. What evidence do they provide to back up their assertion? Do you think that the article by Tara O'Toole and Donald A. Henderson could be viewed as being unnecessarily alarmist about biological weapons? Explain your answer.

4. After reading all the viewpoints in this chapter, do you believe that biological weapons pose a greater, lesser, or equal threat than nuclear weapons? Use the articles to find specific reasons for your answer.

Chapter 2

1. After reading the viewpoints of Frank J. Cilluffo and Jessica Stern, do you believe that knowing the source of a potential biological terrorist act—either foreign or domestic—is important in formulating America's strategic response? Why or why not? What elements of a counterterrorism strategy focused on foreign threats might be different from a strategy focused on domestic terrorists? What elements would be the same?

2. Wendy Orent wonders about the wisdom of trusting Russian scientists, but sees little alternative. Do you see any alternatives to the program she describes in which the United States works with and pays Russian scientists and funds research programs? Are such programs foolish or unavoidable? Explain.

3. After reading the viewpoints by Wendy Orent and Edward Hammond, consider what you would find more disturbing: Incontrovertible evidence that Russia was secretly creating biolog-

ical weapons in violation of the Biological Weapons Convention, or evidence that the United States was doing so. Explain your answer.

Chapter 3

1. Some observers believe that efforts to prepare for bioterrorism and biological warfare might have a beneficial "double effect" in that they might help create solutions to other public health problems as well. After reading the viewpoints of David Stipp and Katherine Eban, do you believe this to be the case? Explain why or why not, citing the viewpoints.

2. Lawrence O. Gostin quotes from John Marshall Harlan on the importance of balancing the common good and individual civil liberties. Does the fact that he cites a Supreme Court justice lend credence to his arguments? Where do you think the "balance" between public health and individual liberty should be? Explain your answers.

3. Twila Brase criticizes the background and record of Lawrence O. Gostin as part of her arguments against law reforms Gostin has proposed. What exactly do her criticisms consist of? Do they constitute an unfair personal attack, or do they have convincing relevance to her arguments? Explain.

4. After reading the viewpoints of Louis Warren, Steven Black, and Paul W. Ewald, consider what you would do if you were presented the option of taking the smallpox vaccine. Would you accept the personal risks? Why or why not? Would your reaction be much different if smallpox vaccinations were mandatory instead of voluntary? Explain your answer.

Chapter 4

1. The Council for a Livable World argues that the Biological Weapons Convention Protocol could be improved, but it is better than no protocol at all. Do you agree, or is a flawed agreement worse than none? Defend your answer.

2. What objections does John R. Bolton make concerning the Biological Weapons Convention Protocol? Which objections do you consider to be the strongest? The weakest? Defend your answer.

3. After reading the viewpoints by David G. Gompert and Thomas Graham Jr., what do you think the official policy of the United States should be regarding nuclear weapons? Should the United States explicitly say such weapons would be used in the event of a biological weapons attack? If you had the choice, would you

drop nuclear weapons on a country that had used biological weapons? Explain why or why not.

4. Donald A. Henderson personally played a leading role in the international campaign to wipe out smallpox. Do you believe his personal history makes him unduly biased in favor of destroying the remaining virus stocks, as Joshua Micah Marshall suggests, or does it lend his views greater credence? Explain your answer.

Organizations to Contact

The editors have compiled the following list of organizations concerned with the issues debated in this book. The descriptions are derived from materials provided by the organizations. All have publications or information available for interested readers. The list was compiled on the date of publication of the present volume; the information provided here may change. Be aware that many organizations take several weeks or longer to respond to inquiries, so allow as much time as possible.

American Legislative Exchange Council (ALEC)
910 17th St. NW, 5th Floor, Washington, DC 20006
(202) 466-3800
website: www.alec.org

ALEC is a bipartisan membership organization of conservative state legislators who believe in limited government. Its website includes information on its initiatives, including its opposition to proposed public health laws that ALEC believes gives government too much power.

Arms Control Association (ACA)
1726 M St. NW, Washington, DC 20036
(202) 463-8270 • fax: (202) 463-8273
e-mail: aca@armscontrol.org • website: www.armscontrol.org

The ACA is a national membership organization that works to educate the public and promote effective arms control policies. It publishes the magazine *Arms Control Today*. Documents and articles on biological weapons and the Biological Weapons Convention can be found on its website.

Biohazard News (BHN)
925 Lakeville St., P.O. Box 251, Petaluma, CA 94952
e-mail: info@biohazardnews.net
website: www.biohazardnews.net

BHN is a volunteer-run organization dedicated to providing the public with timely information about the threat of biological terrorism, which it believes to be one of the most serious threats to America's national security. It publishes a free newsletter and maintains a website that includes interviews and information on biological weapons and terrorist groups.

Brookings Institution
1775 Massachusetts Ave. NW, Washington, DC 20036
(202) 797-6000 • fax: (202) 797-6004
e-mail: brookinfo@brook.edu • website: www.brookings.org

The institution, founded in 1927, is a think tank that conducts research and education in foreign policy, economics, government, and the social sciences. Its publications include the quarterly *Brookings Review*, periodic *Policy Briefs*, and books including *Protecting the American Homeland*.

Center for Law and the Public's Health
Hampton House, Room 582, 624 North Broadway, Baltimore, MD 21205
(410) 955-7624
e-mail: jhodge@jhsph.edu • website: www.publichealthlaw.net

The center is a resource for practical and scholarly information on public health law. Reports and model legislation on legal issues related to biological warfare and terrorism can be found on its website.

Center for Nonproliferation Studies
Monterey Institute of International Studies
460 Pierce St., Monterey, CA 93940
(831) 647-4154 • fax: (831) 647-3519
e-mail: cns@miis.edu • website: http://cns.miis.edu

The center researches all aspects of nonproliferation and works to combat the spread of biological weapons and other weapons of mass destruction. The center provides research databases and has multiple reports, papers, speeches, and congressional testimony online. Its main publication is *The Nonproliferation Review*, which is published three times per year.

Center for Strategic and International Studies (CSIS)
1800 K St. NW, Suite 400, Washington, DC 20006
(202) 887-0200 • fax: (202) 775-3199
website: www.csis.org

The center works to provide world leaders with strategic insights and policy options on current and emerging global issues. It publishes books, including *Combating Chemical, Biological, Radiological, and Nuclear Terrorism*, the *Washington Quarterly*, a journal on political, economic, and security issues, and other publications including reports that can be downloaded from its website.

Centers for Disease Control and Prevention (CDC)
1600 Clifton Rd., Atlanta, GA 30333
(800) 311-3435
e-mail: netinfo@cdc.gov • website: www.cdc.gov

The CDC is the government agency charged with protecting the public health of the nation by preventing and controlling diseases and by responding to public health emergencies. Programs of the CDC include the National Center for Infectious Diseases, which publishes the journal *Emerging Infectious Diseases*. Information on potential biological warfare agents, including anthrax and small-pox, is available on the CDC website.

Chemical and Biological Arms Control Institute
2111 Eisenhower Ave., Suite 302, Alexandria, VA 22314
(703) 739-1538 • fax: (703) 739-1525
e-mail: cbaci@cbaci.org • website: www.cbaci.org

The institute is a nonprofit organization that supports arms control and nonproliferation, particularly of biological and chemical weapons. In addition to conducting research, the institute plans meetings and seminars and assists in the implementation of weapons-control treaties. Its publications include *The Dispatch*, published bi-monthly, and numerous fact sheets, monographs, and reports.

Federation of American Scientists
FAS Chemical and Biological Arms Control Program
1717 K St. NW, Washington, DC 20036
(202) 546-3300 • fax: (202) 675-1010
e-mail: fas@fas.org • website: www.fas.org/bwc

The Federation of American Scientists is a privately funded, non-profit organization engaged in analysis and advocacy on science, technology, and public policy for global security. Its Chemical and Biological Arms Control Program works to prevent the development and use of biological weapons. The federation requests that students and other researchers first investigate the resources available on its website, such as the paper *Biological Weapons and "Bioter-rorism" in the First Years of the 21st Century*, before requesting further information.

Food and Drug Administration (FDA)
5600 Fishers Ln., Rockville, Maryland 20857
(888) 463-6332
website: www.fda.gov/oc/opacom/hottopics/bioterrorism.html

The FDA is a federal government public health agency that monitors the safety of the nation's foods and medicines. Its website includes a special section focusing on biological terrorism, including information on anthrax, how to handle suspicious letters, and food safety.

Henry L. Stimson Center
11 Dupont Circle NW, 9th Floor, Washington, DC 20036
(202) 223-5956 • fax: (202) 238-9604
website: www.stimson.org

The Henry L. Stimson Center is an independent public policy institute committed to finding and promoting innovative solutions to the security challenges confronting the United States and other nations. The center directs the Chemical and Biological Weapons Nonproliferation Project, which serves as a clearinghouse of information related to the monitoring and implementation of the 1972 Biological Weapons Convention. The center produces reports, papers, and books on policy on biological and other weapons of mass destruction.

Johns Hopkins Center for Civilian Biodefense Strategies
111 Market Place, Suite 830, Baltimore, MD 21202
(410) 223-1667 • fax: (410) 223-1665
website: www.hopkins-biodefense.org

The center is an independent, nonprofit organization of the Johns Hopkins Bloomberg School of Public Health and the School of Medicine. It works to prevent the development and use of biological weapons and to advocate medical and public health policies that would minimize the damage of biological warfare. It does not provide clinical care or medical advice to individuals. It produces the journals *Biodefense Quarterly* and *Biosecurity and Bioterrorism*. Articles, reports, and other resources are available on its website.

Sunshine Project
101 West 6th St., Suite 607, Austin, TX 78701
(512) 494-0545
e-mail: tsp@sunshine-project.org
website: www.sunshine-project.org

The Sunshine Project is an international nongovernmental organization that works to avert the dangers of new weapons stemming from advances in biotechnology. It conducts research and issues reports on biological weapons research in Germany, the United States, and other countries. These reports and other information on biological weapons can be downloaded from its website.

U.S. Department of State, Bureau of Nonproliferation
Public Communications Division
2201 C St. NW, Washington, DC 20520
(202) 647-6575
website: www.state.gov/t/np

The Bureau of Nonproliferation leads U.S. efforts to prevent the spread of weapons of mass destruction, including biological weapons. The bureau has primary responsibility for leadership in the interagency process for nonproliferation issues; leads major nonproliferation negotiations and discussions with other countries; and participates in all nonproliferation-related dialogues. Its website offers speeches and news briefings on U.S. foreign policy related to biological weapons.

Websites

ACP-ASIM Online Bioterrorism Resources
www.acponline.org/bioterro

The American College of Physicians-American Society of Internal Medicine (ACP-ASIM) is the nation's largest medical specialty society. Its Bioterrorism Resources webpage includes medical information on anthrax, smallpox, and other biological agents.

All the Virology on the WWW
www.virology.net

All the Virology on the WWW is the leading Internet site for information on viruses. It includes a special section on biological warfare.

Anthrax Vaccine Immunization Program
www.anthrax.osd.mil

The official U.S. Department of Defense anthrax information website provides news and documents related to anthrax and the military vaccination programs.

Defense Threat Reduction Agency
www.dtra.mil

Part of the U.S. Department of Defense, this agency manages America's chemical and biological defense efforts. The website contains information on their programs and initiatives.

Joint Program Office for Biological Defense

www.jpobd.net

The website provides information on U.S. Department of Defense efforts to develop biological detection systems, medical diagnostics, and countermeasures for American military personnel.

NOVA's Bioterror Series

www.pbs.org/wgbh/nova/bioterror

The companion website to a 2001 episode of the public television series *NOVA*, it features interviews with bioterrorism experts and interactive presentations on the biological warfare threat.

Bibliography of Books

Ken Alibek with Stephen Handelman	*Biohazard: The Chilling True Story of the Largest Covert Biological Weapons Program in the World—Told from Inside by the Man Who Ran It.* New York: Random House, 1999.
Wendy Barnaby	*The Plague Makers: The Secret World of Biological Warfare.* New York: Continuum, 1999.
British Medical Association	*Biotechnology, Weapons, and Humanity.* Amsterdam: Harwood Academic Publishers, 1999.
Richard Butler	*The Greatest Threat: Iraq, Weapons of Mass Destruction and the Growing Crisis in Global Security.* New York: Public Affairs, 2000.
W. Seth Carus	*The Threat of Bioterrorism.* Washington, DC: National Defense University, Institute for National Strategic Studies, 1997.
Alan B. Cobb	*Biological and Chemical Weapons: The Debate over Modern Warfare.* New York: Rosen, 2000.
Leonard A. Cole	*The Eleventh Plague: The Politics of Biological and Chemical Warfare.* New York: W.H. Freeman, 1997.
Eric Croddy et al.	*Chemical and Biological Warfare: A Comprehensive Guide for the Concerned Citizen.* New York: Copernicus Books, 2002.
Malcolm Dando	*Biological Warfare in the 21st Century: Biotechnology and the Proliferation of Biological Weapons.* New York: Macmillan, 1994.
Malcolm Dando	*Preventing Biological Warfare: The Failure of American Leadership.* New York: Palgrave Macmillan, 2002.
Stephen L. Endicott	*The United States and Biological Warfare: Secrets from the Early Cold War and Korea.* Bloomington: Indiana University Press, 1998.
Elizabeth A. Fenn	*Pox Americana: The Great Smallpox Epidemic of 1776–1782.* New York: Hill and Wang, 2001.
William H. Frist	*When Every Moment Counts: What You Need to Know About Bioterrorism from the Senate's Only Doctor.* Lanham, MD: Rowman & Littlefield, 2002.
Laurie Garrett	*Betrayal of Trust: The Collapse of Global Public Health.* New York: Hyperion, 2000.

Kathlyn Gay

Silent Death: The Threat of Chemical and Biological Terrorism. Brookfield, CT: Twenty-First Century Books, 2001.

Lawrence O. Gostin

Public Health Law: Power, Duty, Restraint. Berkeley: University of California Press, 2001.

Jeanne Guillemin

Anthrax: The Investigation of a Deadly Outbreak. Berkeley: University of California Press, 2001.

Khidhir Hamza
with Jeff Stein

Saddam's Bombmaker: The Terrifying Inside Story of the Iraqi Nuclear and Biological Weapons Agenda. New York: Scribner, 2000.

Sheldon H. Harris

Factories of Death: Japanese Biological Warfare, 1932–1945, and the American Cover-Up. New York: Routledge, 1994.

Kenneth V. Iserson

Demon Doctors: Physicians as Serial Killers. Tucson, AZ: Galen Press, 2002.

Stuart E. Johnson, ed.

The Niche Threat: Deterring the Use of Chemical and Biological Weapons. Washington, DC: National Defense University, 1997.

Joshua Lederberg, ed.

Biological Weapons: Limiting the Threat (BCSIA Studies in International Security). Cambridge, MA: MIT Press, 1999.

Herbert M. Levine

Chemical & Biological Weapons in Our Times. New York: Franklin Watts, 2000.

Tom Mangold
and Jeff Goldberg

Plague Wars: A True Story of Biological Warfare. New York: St. Martin's Press, 2000.

Judith Miller,
Stephen Engelberg,
and William J. Broad

Germs: Biological Weapons and America's Secret War. New York: Simon & Schuster, 2001.

Michael T. Osterholm
and John Schwartz

Living Terrors: What America Needs to Know to Survive the Coming Bioterrorist Catastrophe. New York: Delacorte, 2000.

Richard Preston

The Demon in the Freezer. New York: Random House, 2002.

Lawrence P. Pringle

Chemical and Biological Warfare: The Cruelest Weapons. Springfield, NJ: Enslow, 2000.

Ed Regis

The Biology of Doom: The History of America's Secret Germ Warfare Project. New York: Henry Holt, 1999.

Scientific American, ed.

Understanding Germ Warfare, New York: Warner Books, 2002.

Jessica Stern

The Ultimate Terrorists. Cambridge, MA: Harvard University Press, 2001.

Tim Trevan — *Saddam's Secrets: The Hunt for Iraq's Hidden Weapons.* North Pomfret, VT: Trafalgar Square, 1999.

Jonathan B. Tucker — *Scourge: The Once and Future Threat of Smallpox.* New York: Atlantic Monthly Press, 2001.

Jonathan B. Tucker, ed. — *Toxic Terror: Assessing Terrorist Use of Chemical and Biological Weapons* (BCSIA Studies in International Security). Cambridge, MA: MIT Press, 2000.

Simon M. Whitby — *Biological Warfare Against Crops.* New York: Palgrave Macmillan, 2002.

Raymond A. Zilinskas, ed. — *Biological Warfare: Modern Offense and Defense.* Boulder, CO: Lynne Rienner, 1999.

Index